MULTICULTURAL TEACHER EDUCATION:

AN ANNOTATED BIBLIOGRAPHY OF SELECTED RESOURCES

Volume III

Compiled By

Marianne Lee

University of Southern California

Prepared for the Project,
Knowledge Interpretation Program:
Training Educators to Provide Educational Equity

Frank H. Klassen, Project Director
Donna M. Gollnick, Principal Investigator
Kobla I. M. Osayande, Program Assistant

Commission on Multicultural Education
American Association of Colleges for Teacher Education
Washington, D.C.

1980

AMERICAN ASSOCIATION OF COLLEGES FOR TEACHER EDUCATION

This material does not necessarily reflect the viewpoints of the American Association of Colleges for Teacher Education (AACTE). AACTE is printing this document to stimulate discussion, study, and experimentation of multicultural education among educators.

This publication was prepared with funding from the National Institute of Education, U.S. Department of Health, Education, and Welfare under contract no. NIE-R-78-0015. The opinions expressed in this publication do not necessarily reflect the positions or policies of NIE or HEW.

Second Printing, 1981
Initially Published 1980 by the
American Association of Colleges for Teacher Education
Suite 610, One Dupont Circle, Washington, D.C. 20036
Printed in the United States of America

Library of Congress Catalog Card Number: 80-80105
Standard Book Number: 0-89333-017-5

FOREWORD

Multicultural education is education which values cultural pluralism. Multicultural education rejects the view that schools should seek to melt away cultural differences or the view that schools should merely tolerate cultural pluralism. Instead, multicultural education affirms that schools should be oriented toward the cultural enrichment of all children and youth through programs rooted to the preservation and extension of cultural alternatives. Multicultural education recognizes cultural diversity as a fact of life in American society, and it affirms that this cultural diversity is a valuable resource that should be preserved and extended. It affirms that major education institutions should strive to preserve and enhance cultural pluralism.

Multicultural education programs for teachers are more than special courses or special learning experiences grafted onto the standard program. The commitment to cultural pluralism must permeate all areas of the educational experience provided for prospective teachers.

So stated AACTE's first Commission on Multicultural Education in 1972. As a result of the Commission's efforts, the standards of the National Council for Accreditation of Teacher Education (NCATE) were revised to include a single standard on multicultural education in 1977. These standards also include references to multicultural education in 14 of the remaining 29 standards for basic teacher education progams and in five of the remaining 39 standards for advanced programs.

As we enter a new decade, the Commission reaffirms its commitment to multicultural education and equal educational opportunity for all students. As the interdependency of nations and people around the world accelerates, the need to prepare educators to be aware of, understand, accept, and function effectively in settings and with people culturally different from themselves is more critical than ever. As teacher educators, we can not neglect our responsibility to develop programs that reflect the multicultural realities of the United States and the world.

One of the Commission's program goals is to assist institutions, agencies, and organizations in the preparation of educational personnel for a pluralistic society and an interdependent world. With the support of a NIE-funded project, Knowledge Interpretation Program: Training Educators to Provide Educational Equity, the Commission has prepared four documents to assist teacher education institutions in the process of designing and redesigning multicultural education programs. Volume III of this series, this bibliography is a compilation of resources and reference materials for possible use in preservice, inservice, and graduate classes. The other three documents are:

Vol. I   Multicultural Teacher Education: Preparing Educators to Provide Educational Equity. A collection of nine papers that recommend strategies for the implementation of multicultural education. Also examined are selected issues, including bidialectal education, learning styles, interpersonal skills training, and disproportionate minority suspension.

Vol. II Multicultural Teacher Education: Case Studies of Thirteen Programs. A collection of case studies based on data from site visits to 13 institutions that varied in size, geographical region, and ethnic and racial composition of the student and community populations. The collection presents alternative strategies for implementing multicultural teacher education programs.

Vol. IV Multicultural Teacher Education: Guidelines for Implementation. A set of guidelines to be used in planning and evaluating multicultural teacher education programs. These guidelines go beyond the minimum requirements of the NCATE standards toward designing exemplary teacher education programs that reflect a commitment to multicultural education and the provision of educational equity.

Edmund J. Cain
Chair, Commission on
 Multicultural Education
Dean, College of Education
University of Nevada, Reno

TABLE OF CONTENTS

Section   Page

      FOREWORD..iii

      ACKNOWLEDGEMENTS.......................................vi

      INTRODUCTION..1

I   REFERENCE RESOURCES.....................................3

      Part 1: Bibliographies..................................3
      Part 2: Concept References.............................14
      Part 3: Directories....................................38
      Part 4: Evaluation Guidelines, Reports, and Studies....43
      Part 5: Historical References..........................51
      Part 6: Literature and Art References..................57
      Part 7: Models, Manuals, Textbooks, and Activities.....61
      Part 8: Research Studies...............................76

II   PERIODICAL RESOURCES...................................80

      Part 1: Journals and Newsletters.......................80
      Part 2: Funding Resources..............................90
      Part 3: Special Articles and Issues....................95

III   ORGANIZATION RESOURCES................................100

      INDEX...114

ACKNOWLEDGMENTS

This bibliography was compiled during a six-month internship at the American Association of Colleges for Teacher Education (AACTE) as part of my doctoral fellowship in the Program for Minorities and Women sponsored by the National Institute of Education.

My gratitude and appreciation are extended to Donna Gollnick, Associate Director of Multicultural Programs at AACTE, for her guidance and assistance. Many thanks also to Kobla Osayande and Virginia Lowes, research assistants, and to Phyllis Irby who helped with the typing and the word processing.

As an instructor in bilingual/cross-cultural education at the University of Southern California between 1973 and 1978, I developed some contacts and bibliography resources which are included here. I would like to thank Sy Abrego, former director of El Centro Chicano at U.S.C. and the fellowship coordinator, for collaboration and guidance over several years. Last, but not least, thank you, Frank Klassen, Associate Director of AACTE, and Gwendolyn Baker, Chief of the Minorities and Women Program at NIE.

Marianne Lee

INTRODUCTION

In addition to current text resources in books and journals, this bibliography contains information about organizations and programs concerned with multicultural and bilingual education. Resources for private and government funding for program development and research are included because "soft money" (i.e., grants and contracts) provide much of the financial support in this field. In general, text resources are dated 1975 or later; however, in some instances publication dates or page numbers may not be indicated. Periodical and organizational resources are current, as of 1978. When the resource is available through the Educational Resource Information Center (ERIC), code numbers for documents (ED) and for journal articles (EJ) are included. Audio-visual resources are not included in this volume.

Concepts and resources in multicultural and bilingual education are best clarified by those who have intimate and extensive experience in a specific cultural setting. Frequently, such persons or groups do not have access to publication channels. Perhaps they are not aware of the channels or are too weighted down with survival problems to follow the required procedures. Nevertheless, an effort has been made to include materials prepared by ethnic minority members in the present volume.

The National Clearinghouse for Bilingual Education, funded under Title VII, ESEA, and ERIC, the National Institute of Education data base, are available to authors as an avenue for dissemination. Assistance is provided as necessary. Central and regional facilities, clearinghouses and document processing offices are listed in the hope that relevant materials will be forwarded to them.

Section I includes a variety of resources that might be used as references in teacher education courses. These resources include bibliographies, concept references, directories, evaluation guidelines, reports, and research studies. In addition, curricular resources, including course and unit models, teacher's guides and manuals, student textbooks, and classroom activities are included. Finally, an excellent source for developing an understanding and appreciation of an unknown cultural group is through literature, folklores, and history written by members of the cultural groups. A number of such resources are also annotated in this section.

Section II, Periodical Resources, contains addresses of journals and newsletters to which authors can submit articles, monographs, and comments concerning multicultural, bilingual, foreign language, and global education, at any level of the educational system. Funding resources and guides for preparing foreign language, and global education, at any level of the educational system. Funding resources and guides for preparing proposals are also listed in this section. Finally, special articles and thematic issues on multicultural education published by various journals are listed.

Section III lists organizations concerned with one or more aspects or cultural group included in multicultural education. Addresses for these organizations are listed. The goals and activities of some of these organizations are outlined at the end of the section.

The following is a list of acronyms used throughout this document:

AACTE	American Association of Colleges for Teacher Education
CFDA	Catalogue of Federal Domestic Assistance
ERIC	Educational Resource Information Center (NIE)
HEW	Department of Health, Education and Welfare
NIE	National Institute of Education
Title VII	Title VII of the 1968 amendment to the Elementary and Secondary Education Act of 1965, known as the Bilingual Education Act, USOE
Title IX	Title IX of the 1972 Amendments to the Elementary and Secondary Act of 1965, Ethnic Heritage Program, USOE
USOE	U.S. Office of Education

Section I

REFERENCE RESOURCES

Part 1: Bibliographies

An Annotated Bibliography of Title VII French Project-Developed Instructional Materials, 1970-1975. Bedford, NH: National Materials Development Center, 1975. Also available from the National Assessment and Dissemination Center.

Listing of instructional materials developed by Title VII projects for French-English bilingual programs.

Benitez, Mario A. and Villarreal, Lupita. The Education of the Mexican-American: A Selected Bibliography. Rosslyn, VA: National Clearinghouse for Bilingual Education.

Although the focus is on education, this bibliography also covers demographic, legal, sociocultural and linguistic concerns. Approximately 200 periodicals are referenced. Citations include books, monographs, journals, federal and state government documents, federal laws, court decisions, doctoral and master's theses, and ERIC documents. Covers the period from 1896 to 1976.

A Bibliography of Asian and Asian American Books for Elementary School Youngsters. (ED 117-286). Olympia, WA: Department of Public Instruction, 1975. 50 pp.

Developed by the Washington Asian-American Cultural Heritage Program and the Asian-American Education Association, this annotated bibliography for elementary school pupils includes folklore, fiction, history, songs, games, and audio-visual materials; a curriculum supplement and list of publishers are also included.

Blaze, Wayne and Nero, John. College Degrees for Adults--A Comprehensive Guide to Over 120 Programs Featuring Options for Self-Directed Learning. Boston, MA: Beacon Press, 1979. 140 pp.

A guide for the adult seeking higher education who finds it difficult to matriculate in the traditional university of college on-campus degree programs.

California State Department of Education. <u>Bibliography of Instructional Materials for the Teaching of Portuguese</u>. Sacramento, CA: Office of Support Services and Bilingual Education, California State Department of Education, 1976. 61 pp.

Lists instructional materials for the teaching of Portuguese.

Calvin, Richmond; Rasmussen, Karen; and Gollnick, Donna M. <u>Bibliography of Multi-Ethnic Materials</u>. South Bend, IN: Ethnic Studies Heritage Program, Indiana University at South Bend, 1975. 175 pp. (Limited Publication)

Information pertaining to cultural pluralism is presented as it relates to Afro-Americans, Hungarian-Americans, Native Americans, Mexican Americans, and Polish Americans. The list offers a systematic approach in securing culturally pluralistic curricula materials for use in schools, institutions of higher education, and social, civic, and cultural organizations. Materials referenced include bibliographies, biographies, histories, social interpretation, art, drama, fiction, literature, music, and audio-visual materials.

Cardenas, Jose A. <u>Multicultural Education: An Annotated Bibliography</u>. (ED 151-430). San Antonio: Intercultural Development Research Association.

This bibliography was compiled from an ERIC computer search and manual search at various university libraries.

Cohen, David. <u>Multi-Ethnic Media: Selected Bibliographies in Print</u>. Chicago: Office for Library Service to the Disadvantaged, American Library Association, 1975. 35 pp.

This bibliography contains selected resource organizations and is extensively annotated. The material has been collected and updated since 1968, with the assistance and cooperation of the American Association of School Librarians' Committee on Treatment of Minority Groups.

Cotera, Martha P. *Educator's Guide to Selected Chicano Materials and Media Resources*. San Antonio: Intercultural Development Research Association.

This product is not intended to be a comprehensive Chicano bibliography, but rather a selection of useful works for the educator and the social service practitioner. The bibliography is for the most part a buying guide, with the exception of subject areas such as labor, politics, and women. In these areas, where much of the material is in periodical form, periodical materials have been included. (Preface)

Dissemination and Assessment Center for Bilingual Education. *CARTEL: Annotations and Analyses of Bilingual Multicultural Materials*. Austin: Dissemination and Assessment Center for Bilingual Education. Revised periodically.

CARTEL is an informative listing for educators, librarians, and others interested in materials for bilingual multicultural education. The annotations attempt to inform, rather than to recommend or disparage. Annotations are based on the following criteria: (1) published or available in the United States, its territories or possessions; (2) include a source address; (3) used in the education of bilingual children; (4) contribute to staff training for bilingual multicultural program; and (5) further the progress or success of bilingual multicultural education.

Dissemination and Assessment Center for Bilingual Education. *Evaluation Instruments for Bilingual Education: An Annotated Bibliography*. Austin, TX: Dissemination and Assessment Center for Bilingual Education, 1975. 125 pp.

A revised and expanded version, this edition is designed to provide the user with easily accessible information on tests; and to aid in the search for specific instruments.

Duran, Daniel Flores. *A Bilingual and Bicultural Annotated List of Print and Multimedia Resources for the Mexican American Child, Grades 7-12*. Latino Resources Series #3. Madison, WI: University of Wisconsin, 1977. 17 pp. Available from the EEO Office, Wisconsin Department of Public Instruction.

An annotated list of print and multimedia resources for Mexican American children, grades 7-12.

EPIE Institute. <u>Selector's Guide for Bilingual Education Materials: The Status of Programs in Chinese, Japanese, Korean and Vietnamese, Vol. III</u>. New York: Educational Products Information Exchange Institute.

   Guide of educational materials available for bilingual education. Includes evaluations of many published materials.

ERIC/CRESS. <u>American Indian Education: A Selected Bibliography</u>. (ED 145-974). Austin: ERIC-CRESS, National Educational Laboratory Publishers, 1977. 400 pp.

   This bibliography provides a guide to the latest resource material, research findings, and/or development in education related to American Indians. This bibliography is drawn from issues of RIE and CIJE between April 1976 and May 1977.

ERIC/CRESS. <u>Mexican American Education: A Selected Bibliography</u>. (ED 107-478). Austin: National Education Laboratory Publications.

   Bibliography of ERIC abstracts, documents (ED) and journal articles (EJ) about Mexican American education. Original and subsequent supplements are available through ERIC; these include: ED 031-353, ED 048-961, ED 065-217, ED 082-881, and ED 097-187.

ERIC/CRESS. <u>Migrant Education: A Selected Bibliography</u>. (ED 139-549). ERIC/CRESS Supplement No. 7. Austin: National Educational Laboratory Publishers, 1977. 205 pp.

   ERIC abstracts of materials published between January and December, 1976, on migrant education are included in this document. The original and supplements available from ERIC include: ED 028-011, ED 040 002, ED 055 706, ED 075 162, ED 087 599, ED 101 909, and ED 118 292.

Eterovich, Adam S. <u>A Guide and Bibliography to Research on Yugoslavs in the United States and Canada</u>. San Francisco, CA: R&E Research Associates, 112), 1975. 187 pp.

   This guide and bibliography includes genealogy, history, immigration, music, dance, and general interests of Yugoslavs in the United States.

Evans, Edward G.; Abbey, Karin; and Reed, Dennis (comps). Bibliography of Language Arts Materials for Native North Americans. (ED 153-763). Los Angeles: American Indian Studies Center, University of California, 1977. 283 pp.

Resource materials for educators, sociologists, students, and the general public.

Froschl, Merle and Williamson, Jane. Feminist Resources for Schools and Colleges: A Guide to Curricular Materials. (ED 154-809). Old Westbury, NY: The Feminist Press, 11568), 1977. 67 pp.

Feminist Resources is an annotated bibliography of nonsexist books, pamphlets, articles and other materials for teachers and students, preschool through higher education.

Giese, James. Multicultural Education: A Functional Bibliography for Teachers. Omaha, NB: Center for Urban Education, The University of Nebraska at Omaha, 1977. 41 pp.

This bibliography includes materials to aid the teacher in developing units about ethnic groups. Special consideration was given materials that emphasized group values, social institutions such as the family and child rearing, and such other topics as community, neighborhood, work and jobs.

Gonzales, Joe R. (materials coordinator). Spanish/English and Native American/English Bibliography. (ED 158-955) Albuquerque, NM: Southwest Bilingual Education Training Resource Center, 1977. 99 pp.

Includes current representative English, Spanish, and Native American bilingual education sources.

Hagel, Phyllis (comp). Resource Guide for New England Libraries. Bedford, NH: National Materials Development Center.

Resource guide of French materials.

Heisley, Michael (comp). An Annotated Bibliography of Chicano Folklore from the Southwestern United States. Los Angeles, CA: The Regents of the University of California, 1977. 190 pp.

    Produced for and distributed by the Center for the Study of
    Comparative Folklore and Mythology, University of California,
    Los Angeles, as part of the project "The Traditional Arts and
    Oral History of Chicanos of Greater Los Angeles, Caifornia."
    This project was funded by the Ethnic Heritage Studies
    Program, USOE.

Inglehart, Babette F. and Mangione, Anthony R. *The Image of Pluralism in American Literature*. New York, NY: Institute on Pluralism and Group Identity of the American Jewish Committee.

    An annotated bibliography on the American experience of European ethnic groups.

Kennicott, Patrick C. *The Study of Black American Rhetoric: An Annotated Bibliography*. New York: Speech Communication Module, ERIC Clearinghouse on Reading and Communication Skills, 1975. 4 pp.

    Twenty-nine entries focusing on Black American oral discourse, based on collected works, analysis and articles.

Kotler, Greta; Kuncaitis, Violetta; and Hart, Elinor *Bibliography of Ethnic Heritage Studies Program Materials*. Washington, DC: National Center for Urban Ethnic Affairs and the National Education Association (NEA), 1976.

    Bibliography of materials developed by projects which received Federal Ethnic Heritage Studies Program grants during the fiscal years 1974-75 and 1975-76. Entries are listed by state. There is brief description of the material and an address where more information or the material itself may be obtained. Slides, video tapes, films and curriculum modules are included.

Levy, Jack. *Bibliography on Multicultural/Multilingual Education*. Alexandria, VA: National Clearinghouse for Bilingual Education, 1979.

    This bibliography includes a partially annotated listing of resources for multicultural and multilingual education.

Leyba, Charles F. *Bibliography: Bilingual Education*. Los Angeles, CA: California State University, 1975.

    This bibliography contains 240 entries: books, reports, periodical literatures, conference presentations, written or published between 1967 and 1972.

Leyba, Charles F. *A Brief Bibliography on Teacher Education and Chicanos*. (ED 090-147). 1974.

Twenty-five references are presented from the ERIC's Resources in Education. The entries deal with teacher education aspects of Chicano education. It includes entries on such issues as the migrant condition, counseling, bilingual education, recruitment of Spanish speaking college students, cultural awareness, and value conflicts of Mexican Americans.

Mallea, John R. and Shea, Edward C. (eds) *Multiculturalism and Education: A Select Bibliography*. Toronto, Ontario: Ontario Institute for Studies in Education and the Ontario Ministry of Culture and Recreation, 1979. 290 pp.

This bibliography includes references in ten categories: plural societies, culture and education, language and education, minorities and education, race and education, ethnicity and education, immigration and education, attitudes and education, multicultural education, and audiovisual materials.

Mankato Minority Group Studies Center. *A Model Program in Multi-Ethnic Heritage Studies: Native American Resources. Annotated Bibliography of Print and Non-Print Materials*. Mankato, MN: Minority Group Study Center, Mankato State College, 1975. 76 pp.

Annotated bibliography arranged by names of the tribes, nations or geographic areas as well as by the curriculum content (e.g., legends, religion).

Mathieson, Moria B. *A Brief Bibliography on Teacher Education and American Indians*. (ED 090-146). 1974.

This bibliography consists of 30 citations of documents reported in Research in Education, all of which deal with teacher education aspects of American Indian education.

Midwest Center for Equal Educational Opportunity. *Multi-Ethnic Bibliography and Supplements, 1974-1977*. Columbia, MO: University of Missouri.

The original annotated bibliography and its subsequent supplements of multi-ethnic curriculum materials, was compiled by the Midwest Center for Equal Educational Opportunity, University of Missouri (Columbia). It is organized by type of material including 16mm films, filmstrips, sound recordings, photo aids, learning kits and packets, simulations and games, booklets and books.

Ministry of Education and Ministry of Culture and Recreation. *Resource List for a Multiculture Society*. Ontario, Canada: Ministry of Education and the Ministry of Culture and Recreation, 1976. 626 pp.

This bibliography is the product of four months' work done by four students on an Ontario Government Experience '76 Project that was funded jointly by the Ministry of Education and the Ministry of Culture and Recreation. It includes a list of multicultural resource materials available in English for the use of teachers and community groups wishing to initiate programs leading to a greater understanding of others.

National Audiovisual Center, National Archives and Records Services. *A Reference List of Audiovisual Materials Produced by the United States Government*. Washington, DC: National Audiovisual Center Reference Section, General Services Administration, 1978. 350 pp.

A list of over 6,000 audiovisual materials selected from over 10,000 programs produced by 175 government agencies covering a wide range of subjects. Education is one of the major topics included in the Center's collection.

Nichols, Margaret S. and O'Neill, Peggy. *Multicultural Resources for Children*. (ED 152-394). Stanford, CA: Multicultural Resources, 1977.

A bibliography of materials for preschool through elementary school in the areas of Black, Spanish-speaking, Asian American, Native American, and Pacific Island cultures.

Peterson, Reece L. and Bass, Kathy. *Mainstreaming: A Working Bibliography*. Minneapolis: National Support Systems Project, 1977. 66 pp.

This bibliography is a compilation of sources and references related to mainstreaming.

Pulles, Patrice. *A Bilingual & Bicultural Annotated List of Print and Multimedia Resources for the Mexican American Child, Grades K-6*. Madison, WI: Wisconsin Department of Public Instruction, Equal Educational Opportunity, 1977. 16 pp.

This annotated resource listing is the first of a series of four informative listings for educators, librarians and others interested in materials for the Mexican-Americans, Puerto Ricans, and other Latino school children. It was developed by the Latino Communications Project, University of Wisconsin, at Madison.

Purushothaman, M. *The Education of Children of Caribbean Origin: Select Research Bibliography*. Manchester, England: Centre for Information and Advice on Educational Disadvantage, 1978.

This bibliography was initially compiled in connection with a conference on the linguistic needs of West Indian children.

Rosenfelt, Deborah Silverton (ed). *Strong Women: An Annotated Bibliography of Literature for the High School Classroom*. Old Westbury, NY: The Feminist Press, 1976. 56 pp.

This annotated bibliography is for high school teachers and students who want inexpensive supplementary readings by and about women. Included are annotations of anthologies, biographies, drama, novels, short stories, and poetry. The bibliography emphasizes the strengths and accomplishments of women.

Salazar, Theresa. *Bilingual Education: A Bibliography*. Greeley, CO: Bureau of Research Services, University of Northern Colorado, 1974. 118 pp.

Approximately 1600 entries, including books, periodicals, papers, reports, research, curriculum, evaluation instruments, advocacy and legislative information concerning bilingual education in the U.S. and some references to other countries.

Schmidt, Velma E. and McNeill, Earldene. *Cultural Awareness--A Resource Bibliography*. (ED 161-992). Washington, DC: The National Association for the Education of Young Children, 1978. 121 pp.

The books and materials listed in this bibliography reflect the increase in multicultural resources for young children. The majority of them have been used for several years with young children in The Learning Tree in Dallas. Teachers and college students from different cultures have used the adult books and materials in this bibliography and responded with their evaluations. Some of the books with older copyright dates are regarded as classic by many educators.

Smiley-Marquez, Carolyn. *Black Americans: A Selected and Annotated Bibliography*. Santa Fe: Cross Cultural Unit, New Mexico Department of Education, 1975. 22 pp.

For grade levels K-12, this bibliography includes social studies, history, biographies, art, drama, literature, bibliographies, resources, A-V materials and periodicals.

Spache, George D. _Good Reading for the Disadvantaged Reader_. (ED 112-364). Champaign, IL: Garrard Publishing Company, 1975. 311 pp.

Bibliographies included in this volume attempt to direct the formation of personal self image in readers of various ethnic and racial backgrounds, both urban and rural.

Tolzmann, Don Heinrich. _German-Americana: A Bibliography_. Metuchen, NJ: The Scarecrow Press, 1975. 384 pp.

Selective listing of German-American, German, and American books, pamphlets, records, photography, albums, dissertations, government documents, newspapers, and periodical articles.

Torres, George A. _Bibliography: Bilingual/Bicultural Education_. Normal, IL: Illinois State University, Department of Curriculum & Instruction, 1976. Limited Publication.

A list of materials to help in correcting the misconceptions about bilingual education.

University Center for International Studies. _Ethnic Studies Bibliography_. Pittsburgh: University Center for International Studies, University of Pittsburgh, in conjunction with the Pennsylvania Ethnic Heritage Studies Center, 1975. 245 pp.

The computer was used to comb articles from 120 social and ethnic studies journals to provide the reader with this annual comprehensive bibliography. Teachers, researchers, and the general reading audience can select a specific ethnic group or a concept such as immigration or assimilation and be directed to the major articles written yearly on the subject.

Zurawski, Joseph W. *Polish American History and Culture: A Classified Bibliography*. Chicago: Polish Museum of America, 1975. 218 pp.

Included are 1700 entries, including some in Polish. Topics deal primarily with Polish-American culture, history, education and Polish-American relations. Translations from Polish literary works are not included.

Part 2: Concept References

Anderson, Theodore and Boyer, Mildred. *Bilingual Schooling in the United States: History, Rationale, Implications and Planning.* Vol. 1 & 2. Detroit, MI: Blaine Ethridge Books, 1976. 297 pp. (Special Collection)

Re-publication of the original work, published in 1970 by Southwest Educational Development Laboratory in Austin, Texas. Contains a new forward by Francesco Cordasco and a supplementary bibliography and appendices.

Anti-Defamation League of B'nai B'rith. *Adolescent Prejudice.* New York: Harper & Row and Author, 1976. 48 pp.

Summary of the proceedings and recommendations of a national invitational conference sponsored by the University of California, Berkeley in January 1976.

Aoki, Ted. *Whose Culture? Whose Heritage?*, Vancouver, B.C., Canada: Center for the Study of Curriculum and Instruction, Faculty of Education, University of British Columbia, 1977. 65 pp.

A summary of a larger report (Canadian Ethnic/Multicultural Content in Program Guides of Provincial and Territorial Departments of Education) submitted to the Canadian Ethnic Studies Advisory Committee in September 1974. That report was a survey of existing social studies curricula. Data sources were the documents for social studies, social science, and history programs published by the provincial and territorial departments on education. Correspondence with these departments provided information on rationales, policy statements, and guidelines for developing ethnic studies.

Arciniega, Tomas A. *Preparing Teachers of Mexican Americans: A Sociocultural and Political Issue.* Austin: National Educational Laboratory Publishers, 1977. 34 pp.

This monograph focuses on the implications that are imperative for teacher preparation programs which purport to serve the needs of the Mexican Americans.

Arnow, Beth. *Bilingual/ESL Programs for Migrant Children*. (ED 134-351). Austin: ERIC-CRESS, National Educational Laboratory Publishers, 1977.

This monograph is concerned with the development of special programs for Spanish speaking migrant children. Because these children are migratory, they have special social and physical needs, and programs developed for them cannot focus solely on academic needs and classroom activities. Comprehensive programs must consider and, if possible, include the family and the community in order to meet the needs of the children as completely as possible.

Asia Society. *Asia in American Textbooks*. New York, NY: The Asia Society, Inc. 1976, 25 pp.

Problems encountered in U.S. education when dealing with and thinking about Asia, its culture, history and people.

Bagley, Christopher. *A Comparative Perspective on the Education of Black Children in Britain*. Manchester, England: Centre for Information and Advice on Educational Disadvantage, 1977. 30 pp. (Limited Publication)

There is some evidence that Black children of West Indian origin in British schools are underachieving relative to their white counterparts. This paper examines these research findings.

Baker, Gwendolyn G.; Hunter, Kathleen A.; Murakishi, Linda J.; Salas, Isabel; and Schlitt, Ann M. *Multicultural Education: Teaching About Minority Women*. (ED 142-509). Special Current Issues Publication. Washington, DC: ERIC Clearinghouse on Teacher Education, 1977. 27 pp.

This eighth in the series of Special Current Issues Publications (SCIP) treats the convergence of two pernicious social maladies--racism and sexism--and suggests implications for teacher education efforts to mitigate these ills.

Banks, James A. *Ethnicity and Schooling: Implications for Dissemination*. Unpublished monograph.

This copyrighted paper was prepared for the conference on ethnic studies dissemination held in November 1978 at the Social Science Education Consortium as the Ethnic Heritage Studies Clearinghouse was being initiated.

Banks, James A. *Teaching Strategies for Ethnic Studies*. Second edition. Boston: Allyn & Bacon, 1979. 482 pp.

This book was designed to help teachers realize the content, strategies, concepts, and resources needed to teach comparative ethnic studies and to integrate ethnic content into the regular curriculum. It is based on the assumption that multiethnic approaches to the teaching of ethnic studies are not only appropriate, but essential.

Baptiste, H. Prentice, Jr. and Baptiste, Mira Lanier. *Multicultural Education: A Synopsis*. Houston: College of Education, University of Houston, 1976, 65 pp.

Selections on the evolvement of multicultural education in American education; definitions, models and issues related to multicultural education and bilingual education. Also included are mini-reviews of critical publications in multicultural education and a glossary of selected terms.

Baptiste, H. Prentice; Baptiste, Mira L.; and Gollnick, Donna M. *Multicultural Teacher Education: Preparing Educators to Provide Educational Equity*, Volume I. Washington, DC: AACTE, 1980.

A collection of nine papers that examine strategies for putting multicultural education into practice in teacher education programs. Specific recommendations for competencies and programs are made by each author.

Barnhardt, Ray. *Being a Native and Becoming a Teacher*. (ED 088-631). Los Angeles, CA: Western Teacher Corps, Recruitment and Technical Resources Center, 1973. 16 pp.

Prepared for a symposium at the annual meeting of the American Anthropological Association in New Orleans, Louisiana.

Barnhardt, Ray. *Cross-Cultural Issues in Alaskan Education*. Fairbanks, AK: Center for Northern Educational Research, University of Alaska at Fairbanks, 1977. 165 pp.

The original idea for this collection grew out of a symposium on native education in Alaska presented by staff and students of the Cross-Cultural Education Development Program (X-CED) at the Society for Applied Anthropology meeting in St. Louis, in March 1976. The intent of this publication is to provide for this broader dissemination and to encourage interaction and exchange of ideas on the issues.

Baroni, Geno and Green, Gerson. <u>Who's Left in the Neighborhood?</u> Washington, DC: National Center for Urban Ethnic Affairs, 1977. 54 pp.

A report on relative conditions in the white, Black and Hispanic working class neighborhoods of older industrial cities in the U.S.

Berry, Mary F. <u>Title IX: A Renewed Commitment.</u> Unpublished paper.

Address delivered at the National Title IX Dissemination Workshop, sponsored by the Council of Chief State School Officers.

Beuf, Ann H. <u>Red Children in White America.</u> Philadelphia: University of Pennsylvania Press, 1977. 150 pp.

Living and working with three Native American tribes, Ann Beuf studied the effects of interpersonal prejudice and institutional racism on 229 preschool children. Using the technique of doll-play and the projective storytelling test, she found that, even on an isolated reservation where young children have little personal contact with whites, racism in the dominant American culture is in itself sufficient to impart status assumptions to a child.

<u>Bilingual Education: Current Perspectives.</u> Arlington, VA: Center for Applied Linguistics, 1978.

Series in five volumes, consisting of essays by different authors and extensive bibliography. Includes volumes for social science, linguistics, law, education, and synthesis.

Boyer, James B. and Boyer, Joe L. (eds) <u>Curriculum and Instruction After Desegregation.</u> Manhattan, KS: AG Press, 1975. 144 pp.

Thirteen brief essays by education specialists representing racial and ethnic diversity from a variety of viewpoints.

Brazziel, William F. <u>Quality Education for All Americans.</u> (ED 095-232). Washington, DC: Howard University Press, 1974. 264 pp.

An assessment of the gains of Black Americans with proposals
for program development in American schools and colleges for
the next 25 years.

Buergenthal, Thomas and Torney, Judith V. International Human
Rights and International Education. Washington, DC: U.S.
National Commission for UNESCO, Department of State, 1976.
211 pp.

The first major scholarly work to be produced under the
sponsorship of the Human Rights Task Force of the U.S.
National Commission for UNESCO. The impetus for its
publication was provided by the promulgation in 1974 of the
UNESCO "Recommendation Concerning Education for International
Understanding, Cooperation and Peace and Education Relating
to Human Rights and Fundamental Freedoms."

Carnegie Council on Policy Studies in Higher Education.
Selective Admissions in Higher Education. (ED 145-775). San
Francisco, CA: Jossey-Bass, Inc., 1977. 256 pp.

Comment and recommendations on public policy, academic policy
and the pursuit of fairness in admissions to higher
education.

Casso, Henry J. Bilingual/Bicultural Education and Teacher
Training. (ED 131-0505). Washington, DC: National
Education Association, in cooperation with the ERIC
Clearinghouse on Teacher Education, 1976, 96 pp.

Bilingual/bicultural education in the United States is
undergoing a renaissance, one of the most important, dynamic,
and dramatic reform movements in the history of American
public education. It has serious implications for minorities
(linguistically and culturally distinct students), for the
majority (monolingual students), for present and future
teachers, and for those educational entities responsible for
preservice and inservice teacher training.

Castaneda, Alfredo; James, Richard L.; and Robbins, Webster. The
Educational Needs of Minority Groups. (ED 118-515).
Lincoln, NB: Professional Educators Publications, 1974.

Three essays written by a Hispanic, a Black, and a Native
American. Bibliographies are included.

Cobbs, Price M. and Winokur, Diane K. *Education for Ethnic and Racial Diversity*. Bellingham, WA: Far West Teacher Corps, Western Washington State College, 1977. 50 pp.

   Prepared by Pacific Management Systems from material developed for a workshop in Multicultural Education sponsored by the Far West Teacher Corps Network. Includes annotated bibliography of books, ERIC documents, journals, and evaluation instruments.

Colangelo, Nicholas; Foxley, Cecelia H.; and Dustin, Dick (eds). *Multicultural Nonsexist Education*. Dubuque, IA: Kendall/Hunt Publishing Co., 1979. 416 pp.

   Incorporates facets of human relations education (i. e., human relations training, multicultural education, nonsexist education and related issues on stereotyping) into a single text.

Commission for Racial Equality. *Teacher Education for a Multicultural Society*. London, England: Commission for Racial Equality, 1978. 71 pp. (Limited Publication)

   A consideration of ways in which the training of British teachers can better equip them in an ethnically and culturally diverse society, and how future patterns of training, preservice and inservice can better recognize this need.

Community Relations Commission. *A Second Chance: Further Education in Multi-Racial Areas*. London, England: Community Relations Commission, Reference and Technical Services Division, 1976. 134 pp.

   A consideration of British adult, vocational and E. S. L. education in intercultural and minority/dominant settings.

Community Relations Commission. *Seen But Not Served: Black Youth and The Youth Service*. London, England: Youth and Community Section, Community Relations Commission, 1977. 43 pp.

   Report of a series of six seminars held in 1975/76 to examine statutory provision for young people from racial minorities.

Cortes, Carlos E. *Multicultural Education: A Global Perspective.* Boulder, CO: ERIC Clearinghouse for Social Science Education, 1977. (Limited Publication)

Monograph examining the relationship of multicultural and global education.

Cortes, Carlos E. *Multicultural Law-Related Education in the Humanities: Preparing Young People for a Future of Constructive Pluralism.* Unpublished Document, 1978. 19 pp.

Prepared for the proceedings of the American Bar Association Symposium, Law and the Humanities: A Design for Elementary Law-Related Education, Chicago, May 20-22, 1978.

Cross, Dolores E.; Baker, Gwendolyn C.; and Stiles, Lindley J. (eds). *Teaching in a Multicultural Society.* New York: The Free Press, 1977. 221 pp.

Designed to advance the multicultural society by helping teachers and their students to learn to respond with intellectual honesty to the multicultural conditions that prevail. Such an objective stems from the authors' common conviction that the school is the forum from which perceptions of movement toward the multicultural society will emerge.

Cullinan, Bernice E. (ed). *Black Dialects & Reading.* (ED 086-949). Urbana, IL: National Council of Teachers of English, 1974. 198 pp.

A review of the state of the art, commissioned by the National Institute of Education and undertaken by the ERIC Clearinghouse on Reading and Communications.

Daniel, Jack L. (ed). *Black Communication--Dimensions of Research and Instruction.* New York: Speech Communication Association, 1974. 203 pp.

Ten essays by Black authors and educators commissioned by the Speech Communication Association and discussed by a task force at Pittsburgh, Pennsylvania in 1972. The purposes of this collection are 1) guidelines and resources for research and teaching in Black communities and 2) resource materials for training institutes.

Daniels, Deborah K. (ed). <u>Education By, For and About African Americans: A Profile of Several Black Community Schools</u>. Lincoln, NE: The Nebraska Curriculum Development Center, University of Nebraska, 1976. 86 pp.

A monograph prepared by the Student Committee of the Study Commission on Undergraduate Education and the Education of Teachers. Some black teachers are shown in action, describing the communities that they serve from the preschool level to college level. Implications for black teachers in black and white teacher training institutions are considered.

Darnell, Frank (ed). <u>Education in the North: The First International Conference on Cross- Cultural Education in the Circumpolar Nations</u>. (ED 092-272). Fairbanks, AK: University of Alaska, Arctic Institute of North America, 1972. 370 pp.

Report of the First International Conference on Cross-Cultural Education in the Circumpolar Nations, August 1969, in Montreal.

Davidson, R. Theodore. <u>Chicano Prisoners: The Key to San Quentin</u>. New York: Holt, Rinehart and Winston, 1974. 195 pp.

Part of a case study series in Cultural Anthropology, written by men and women who have lived in the societies they write about and are professionally trained as observers of human behavior. (General editors: George and Louise Spindler, Stanford University, CA)

Dawson, Martha E. (ed). <u>Are There Unwelcome Guests in Your Classroom?</u> (ED 092-649). Washington, DC: Association for Childhood Education International (ACEI), 71 pp.

One of a three part series, this essay provides information for the non-minority teacher.

Elazar, Daniel, and Friedman, Murray. <u>Moving Up</u>. New York: American Jewish Committee, Institute on Pluralism and Group Identity, 1976. 59 pp.

Ethnic succession in America, with a case history from the Philadelphia School System.

Gappa, Judith M. Improving Equity in Postsecondary Education: New Directions for Leadership. (ED 154-709). Washington, DC: The National Institute of Education, 1977.

This publication is the final report of a workshop on equity in postsecondary education, sponsored by the National Institute of Eduation, and conducted by the National Center for Higher Education Management Systems (NCHEMS) at Keystone, Colorado, July 17-20, 1977.

Giles, Raymond H., Jr. Black Studies Programs in Public Schools. New York: Praeger Publishers, 1974. 156 pp.

An examination and analysis of ethnic and minority studies programs in the elementary and secondary schools. The author believes that ethnically oriented programs, related to curricula reform and designed to encourage desired attitudes and values, can be developed within the framework of the existing institutional structure of the American educational system.

Giles, Raymond H. The West Indian Experience in British Schools: Multi-Racial Education and Social Disadvantage in London. London, England: Heinemann Educational Books LTD, 1977. 163 pp.

An analysis and description of practices and policies developed by the teaching staffs in selected multiracial schools serving indigenous children from socially disadvantaged backgrounds in the Inner London Education Authority.

Gold, Milton J.; Grant, Carl A.; and Rivlin, Harry N. In Praise of Diversity: A Resource Book for Multicultural Education. Washington, DC: Teacher Corps and Association of Teacher Educators, 1977. 222 pp.

Addresses multiculturalism, the dangers of stereotyping, areas of possible conflict and controversy, and implications for schools. Nine ethnic vignettes describe the experiences in the U.S. of major ethnic and racial groups. Classroom applications of the information included in the book are also presented.

Lippitt, Gordon L. and Hoopes, David S. (eds). Helping Across Cultures. LaGrange Park, IL: Intercultural Network. 80 pp.

Discusses cross-cultural consultation in terms of trends, key issues, guidelines, principles, methods, techniques, and future developments.

Grant, Carl A. Multicultural Education: Commitments, Issues, and Applications. Alexandria, VA: Association For Supervision and Curriculum Development, 1977.

This booklet is the product of ASCD's Multicultural Commission. Beginning with a position statement on multicultural education, the document reflects varying views of a complex concept.

Grant, Carl A. (ed). Sifting and Winnowing: An Exploration of the Relationship Between Multicultural Education and CBTE. Madison, WI: Teachers Corps Associates, University of Wisconsin-Madison, 1975. 253 pp.

An exploration of the relationship between multicultural education and CBTE.

Hall, Gene; Hord, Shirley; and Brown, Gaile (eds). Exploring Issues in Teacher Education: Questions for Future Research. Austin: Communication Services, Education Annex, University of Texas, 1979.

This volume is comprised of 26 topical papers and the remarks of 14 discussants shared at an invitational conference hosted by the UTR&D Center for Teacher Education, January 10-12, 1979.

Hall, Gene (ed). A National Agenda for Research and Development in Teacher Education 1979-1984. Austin: Communication Services, University of Texas, 1979. 86 pp.

This report summarizes the activities and outcomes of a planning project responsible for delineating and prioritizing crucial, researchable issues in teacher education.

Halperin, Michael and Shuman, Pamela. Helping Maltreated Children--School and Community Involvement. St. Louis, MO: The C. V. Mosby Company, 1979. 198 pp.

Designed as a starting kit for people concerned with education's obligation to maltreated children. It speaks to the teacher, administrator or school board member who is concerned about improving the quality of life for children and their families. It addresses interested parent and neighborhood groups who view the school as an integral part of community life with application for professional social service workers who look to the school for assistance in helping their mutual clients.

Harley, Sharon and Terborg-Penn, Rosalyn. <u>The Afro-American Women: Struggles and Images</u>. Port Washington, NY: Kennikat Press, 1978. 130 pp.

The essays in this anthology share several of the variations on the theme of racial and sexual discrimination characterizing the historical plight of Afro American women throughout the history of the United States.

Haro, Carlos Manual. <u>Mexicano/Chicano Concerns and School Desegregation in Los Angeles</u>. Monograph No. 9. (ED 157-643). Los Angeles, CA: University of California, Chicano Studies Center Publication, 1978. 92 pp.

Discussion of desegregation in the second largest school district in the nation involving a Chicano "minority" which is now larger than both the Black and Anglo school population.

Hartley, Mary Elizabeth. <u>Getting Uncle SAM to Enforce Your Civil Rights</u>. Washington, DC: Publications Division, U. S. Commission on Civil Rights, 1979. 44 pp.

Describes how and where to file a complaint concerning civil rights. Also lists agency regional and local offices.

Hoopes, David S.; Pederson, Paul B.; and Renwick, George W. (eds). <u>Overview of Intercultural Education, Training and Research</u>. Vol. I, II, & III. Washington, DC: Society for Intercultural Education, Training, and Research, Georgetown University, 1978.

Vol. I - Contains articles on the basic concepts that constitute the framework for intercultural communication and cross-cultural training. Vol. II - (Training and Education) Ideas and methods are applied, including inter-ethnic and race relations training. Vol. III - (Special Research Areas) Evaluation of intercultural courses and programs.

Hoopes, David S. and Ventura, Paul (ed). <u>Intercultural Sourcebook: Cross-Cultural Training Methodologies</u>. Washington, DC: Society for Intercultural Education, Training and Research (SIETAR), Georgetown University, 1978. 188 pp.

Comprehensive survey of cross-cultural training methods.

Hunter, William A. (ed). <u>Multicultural Education Through Competency-Based Teacher Education</u>. Washington, DC: AACTE, 1974, 276 pp.

Explores multicultural education through the perspectives of Black, Hispanic and Native American educators.

Israel, William I. (ed). <u>Political Issues in Education</u>. Washington, DC: Council of Chief State School Officers, 1978. 156 pp.

Examines political issues in education including the actors involved in the decisions that must be made; the ends sought, and proposals for reaching these ends; reallocations of power, financial support, or other resources to satisfy the varied interests; and action alternatives open to chief state school officers.

Jaramillo, Mari-Luci. <u>Cautions When Working With the Culturally Different Child</u>. (ED 115 622). Paper read at the Teacher Corps Conference, University of Wisconsin at Madison, WI 1973. 24 pp.

Suggestions for teachers and administrators who work with Hispanic children. Topics relate to the child in the classroom, family and community.

Jones, Reginald L. (ed). <u>Mainstreaming and the Minority Child</u>. Reston, VA: Council for Exceptional Children, 1976. 305 pp.

This collection of papers focuses on mainstreaming of the minority child. Includes sections on educational assessment, curriculum issues, and teaching strategies, evaluation and research, and a case study.

King, Edith W. <u>Teaching Ethnic Awareness: Methods and Materials for the Elementary School</u>. Santa Monica: Goodyear Publishing Co., 1980.

A resource on multiethnic education for teachers. Provides background information on why it is important to understand concept and theories about multiethnic education, levels K-6.

Klassen, Frank H. and Gollnick, Donna M. (eds). Pluralism and the American Teacher: Issues and Case Studies. (ED 134-575). Washington, DC: Ethnic Heritage Center for Teacher Education, AACTE, 1977. 252 pp.

A collection of the papers and reports prepared for the Leadership Training Institute, "Multicultural Education in Teacher Education," sponsored by the Ethnic Heritage Center, April 28-30, 1976, in Washington, DC. Part II, entitled "Case Studies on Multicultural Teacher Education" is a description and analysis of six multicultural teacher education programs at various teacher education institutions. The appendix lists selected multicultural resources.

Klassen, Frank H. and Leavitt, Howard B. (eds). Education for Development: Expanding The Role of Teacher Education. Washington, DC: The International Council on Education for Teaching, 1978. 136 pp.

A collection of papers presented at the XXIV World Assembly of the International Council on Education for Teaching held at Lagos, Nigeria in 1977. Educators from around the world discuss their nations' responses to non-traditional programs for children, youth, and adults in changing societies. Case studies of formal and non-formal education programs in the fields of agriculture and rural development, adult and community education, industrial and occupational education, and the utilization of mass media are included.

Kohls, Robert L. Survival Kit For Overseas Living. LaGrange Park, IL: Intercultural Network. 88 pp.

Covers a range of complex personal issues involved in living abroad. It makes one aware of the quantity of cultural baggage one drags around the world.

Levinsohn, Florence H.; Wright, Benjamin D. (eds). School Desegregation: Shadow and Substance. Chicago, IL: The University Chicago Press, 1976, 216 pp.

Sixteen essays by selected authors in response to the question, "Is School desegregation still a good idea?"

Longstreet, Wilma S. Aspects of Ethnicity: Understanding Differences in Pluralistic Classrooms. (ED 162-039). New York: Teachers College Press, Columbia University, 1978. 196 pp.

Consideration of ethnicity in terms of social values, orientation modes, verbal and nonverbal communication, and action researching.

Lopez, Ronald W.; Madrid-Barela, Arturo; and Macias, Reynaldo Flores. Chicanos in Higher Education: Status and Issues. (ED 136-984). Los Angeles: Chicano Studies Center, University of California, 1976. 199 pp.

Synthesis of information presented at the May 1975 symposium on the status of Chicanos in higher education, held at the University of California at Los Angeles. A bibliography is included.

McCormack, Wayne (ed). The Bakke Decision: Implications for Higher Education Admissions. (ED 158-681). Washington, DC: American Council on Education and Association of American Law Schools, 1978. 61 pp.

An analysis of the Bakke decision and the several opinions by the Justices of the Supreme Court. It seeks to assist educators and educational policymakers in understanding the Supreme Court's decision.

The Measure of Poverty: A Report to Congress as Mandated by the Education Amendments of 1974. (ED 126-173). Washington, DC: U.S. Department of HEW, 1976. 162 pp.

Summary of the report made to the U.S. Congress. It deals with the measure of poverty which is used in the formula for allocation of funds under Title I of the Elementary and Secondary Education Act of 1974--the government's official statistical poverty matrix.

Midura, Edmund M. (ed). Blacks and Whites--The Urban Communication Crisis. Washington, DC: Acropolis Books, 1974. 191 pp.

An examination of problems confronting a racially divided society and discussion of attempts being made to ameliorate them. Contributors include nationally known journalists and concerned business and community leaders. This document is a result of the "Baltimore Sun Distinguished Lecture Series," a project of the Department of Journalism, University of Maryland.

Mohr, Paul (ed). <u>Desegregation, Culturalism and Humanism</u>. (ED 125-999). Lincoln, NB: The Curriculum Development Center, University of Nebraska, 1976. 60 pp.

Recognizing that 21 years of trial and error in implementing school desegregation have produced limited results, two public school superintendents express the need for continuous concern for curricular and personnel policies that facilitate desegregation. Several basic assumptions regarding multicultural education are explained.

Morris, Lee; Sather, Greg; and Scull, Susan (eds). <u>Extracting Learning Styles From Social/Cultural Diversity: Studies of Five American Minorities</u>. (ED 158-952). Washington, DC: Southwest Teacher Corps Network, U. S. Office of Education.

Selections by JoAnn Brown (Mind Sets Paper), Bill Burgess (Native American Culture), Carolos Cortes, (Chicano Culture), Janice Hale (Afro-American Culture), Daniel Selakovich (Low-Income White Culture), Benjamin Tong (Asian-American Culture), Bette Hwang (Instructional Units Paper), and Alfredo Castaneda (Epilogue). The authors discuss the uniqueness of cultures, the resultant learning styles, and the implications which these learning styles may have for organizing classroom instruction.

Murray, John. <u>Toronto Educational Governance/Multiuclturalism Case Study</u>. Toronto, Ontario: The Minister of Education, 1977. 175 pp.

Report of a seminar held in October 1976, sponsored by International Management Training for Educational Change and the U. S. Office of Education. Examines strategies used in various Western countries to plan, develop, implement, and manage change. The sub-topics of the seminar were cultural pluralism; management, governance, and finance; career preparation; and early childhood education.

Muse, Ivan D. Preservice Programs for Educational Personnel Going Into Rural Schools. (ED 135-506). Austin, TX: ERIC-CRESS, National Educational Laboratory Publishers. 50 pp.

An overview of problems faced by teachers in rural areas and a survey of past and present training strategies relevant to rural-teacher development. The paper was reviewed by the Rural/Region Education Association.

National Advisory Council on Women's Educational Programs. Educational Equity: The Continuing Challenge. Washington, DC: Author, 1979. 32 pp.

The fourth annual report of women's educational programs.

National Conference of Christians and Jews. Desegregation Without Turmoil: Center for Quality Integrated Education. New York: Author, 1976. 45 pp.

An experience guide, based on a national conference, May, 1976, on the role of the multiracial community coalition in preparing for a smooth transition during desegregation. The U. S. Department of Justice Community Relations Service cosponsored the conference.

National Institute of Education. Desegregation and Education Concerns of the Hispanic Community. Washington, DC: The National Institute of Education, 1977.

The report of a conference held in June 1977 to exchange information and ideas, to discuss selected case studies, and to identify areas of needed research.

National Institute of Education. The Desegregation Literature: A Critical Appraisal. (ED 135-890). Washington, DC: The National Institute of Education, US Department of HEW, 1976. 158 pp.

A synthesis of relevant literature, 1960 through 1976. Three topics are examined: (1) school desegregation and educational inequality, (2) process of interracial schooling, and (3) research on desegregation in school and classroom.

National Institute of Education. Education, Social Science and the Judicial Process: An International Symposium. (ED 135-703). Washington, DC: National Institute of Education 1976. 95 pp.

Seven essays presented at an international symposium in February 1976.

National Institute of Education and New Mexico State University. Minority Women in Research in Education. (ED 148-521). Las Cruces, NM: New Mexico State University, 1978. 60 pp.

Fourteen women, representing six ethnic backgrounds, focused their experience and thinking for three days upon the problem of expanding the role of minority women in educational research. Each of the women brought a particular set of personal characteristics to the composition of the group including ethnicity, subject matter field, geographical background, career ladder achievement, age, and educational affiliation.

National Institute of Education. School Crime and Disruption: Prevention Models. (ED 160-710). Washington, DC: National Institute of Education, 1978. 195 pp.

This anthology is part of the national effort to respond to the school crime problem by gathering and disseminating information on its probable causes and potential solutions.

Osgood, Charles E.; May, William H.; and Miron, Murray S. Cross-Cultural Universals of Affective Meaning. Urbana: University of Illinois Press, 1975. 460 pp.

Authors from 25 countries and varied geographic areas consider cross-cultural universals in the human experience in an effort to cross culture and language barriers.

Pantoja, Antonia; Blourock, Barbara; and Bowman, James (eds). Badges & Indicia of Slavery: Cultural Pluralism Redefined. (ED 127-391). Lincoln, NB: Study Commission on Undergraduate Education and the Education of Teachers, 1975. 225 pp.

Includes four papers and one extensive bibliography. Separate sections examine Blacks, Chicanos, education, ethnicity, history, homosexuals, language, Native Americans, neighborhoods, politics, Puerto Ricans, religion, and women.

Phelps, Stanlee, and Austin, Nancy. The Assertive Woman. San Luis Obispo, CA: Impact Publishers, 1975. 182 pp.

Practical suggesions for the passive, compassionate woman, including an A-Q (assertiveness quotient) test, checklists, resources, examples and exercises.

Pifer, Alan. Black Progress: Achievement, Failure, and an Uncertain Future. (ED 154-096). Reprint from the 1977 Annual Report of Carnegie Corporation of New York. New York: Carnegie Corporation, 1977. 11 pp.

Monograph and commentary on several major publications about the progress of Blacks in this country..

Pottker, Jannice and Fischel, Andrew (eds). Sex Bias in the Schools. Second Printing. Cranbury, NJ: Associated University Presses, 1978. 100 pp.

The text is divided into 10 major sections: pre-school and elementary education; secondary education; textbooks; role formation (occupational, social, and political); counseling; policymakers; higher education; state and local studies of sex bias in public education; opinion polls; and sex differences in educational attainment.

Pratte, Richard. Pluralism in Education. Springfield, IL: Charles C. Thomas, 1979. 201 pp.

Focuses on the conflict that surrounds cultural pluralism and on how cultural pluralism affects education and schooling. The essays provide a working knowledge of cultural pluralism and its bearing on educational policies and practices.

President's Commission on Foreign Language and International Studies. President's Commission on Foreign Language and International Studies: Background Papers and Studies. Washington, DC: Author, 1979. 312 pp.

This volume supplements the final report of the President's Commission on Foreign Language and International Studies, Strength Through Widsom: A Critique of U. S. Capability, published November 1979.

President's Commission on Foreign Language and International Studies. Strength Through Wisdom: A Critique of U. S. Capability. Washington, DC: U.S. Government Printing Office, 1979. 155 pp.

Final report after a year of hearings and deliberations by the Commission. Includes recommendations.

Pusch, Margaret D. Multicultural Education: A Cross-Cultural Training Approach. LaGrange Park, IL: Intercultural Network. 300 pp.

A comprehensive manual that shows how to apply the experiential learning methods of cross-cultural training to the training of teachers in multicultural education.

Frazier, Nancy and Sadker, Myra. Sexism in School and Society. New York: Harper and Row, 1973.

Provides an overview of the basic issues related to sexism in education. It includes an annotated bibliography and a questionnaire on sex bias in education.

Schulman, Jay; Shatter, Aubrey; and Ehrlich, Rosalie (eds). Pride and Protest: Ethnic Roots in America. New York: Dell Publishing, 1977, 336 pp.

This anthology provides significant insights into the personal and social complexities of the ethnic experiences of the sixties.

Seitz, Victoria. Social Class and Ethnic Group Differences in Learning to Read. Newark, DE: International Reading Association, 1975. 35 pp.

This monograph is part of a series on the development of the reading process. It was developed as a result of the 1974 Interdisciplinary Institute in Reading and Child Development at the University of Delaware.

Simonson, Michael R. Global Awareness in the Curriculum. Ames, IA: Research Institute for Studies in Education, Iowa State University, 1976.

Edited proceedings of a conference on global awareness in the curriculum held in June 1975, by the College of Education at Iowa State University are presented in this document.

Sotomayor, Frank. <u>Para Los Ninos--For the Children: Improving Education for Mexican Americans.</u> Washington, DC: U.S. Commission on Civil Rights.

This report is drawn from the published and unpublished findings of the Mexican American Education Study conducted by the Commission between 1969 and 1974. Additional material was obtained from interviews with students, parents, and educators throughout the Southwest. The report deals with the education of Mexican Americans in Arizona, California, Colorado, New Mexico, and Texas, but is applicable to Mexican Americans in other parts of the U.S. Case histories are presented informally to illustrate the first day of school, what students feel, what teachers expect, what schools are doing, and bilingual exercises. The publication is available in Spanish as well as English.

Stewart, Edward C. <u>American Cultural Patterns: A Cross-Cultural Perspective.</u> Washington, DC: Society for Intercultural Education, Training, and Research, Georgetown University. 104 pp.

Cross-cultural analysis of American cultural assumptions and values and a comparison of cultural patterns of thinking and behaving.

Sutman, Francis X.; Sandstrom, Eleanor L.; and Shoemaker, Francis. <u>Educating Personnel for Bilingual Settings: Present and Future.</u> (ED 165-961). Washington, DC: AACTE, 1979. 92 pp.

Includes a literature review of bilingual teacher education and guidelines for program development. In addition, multilingual education in the Philadelphia School District is described. Appendices include competencies for teachers and available resources.

<u>Teacher Education in the United States: The Responsibility Gap.</u> (ED 123-196). Lincoln, NB: Study Commission on Undergraduate Education and the Education of Teachers, University of Nebraska, 1976. 224 pp.

This national project brought together more than 50 nationally selected Commission members and consultants to develop and refine the essays included in this document.

Thompson, Thomas (ed). *The Schooling of Native America*. (ED 168-751). Washington, DC: AACTE, 1978. 199 pp.

The collection of ten essays by Native Americans who are involved in Indian education. Appendices include "A Chronology of Pivotal Dates in Indian Education 1568-1975," capsule profile of Indian education organizations, a list of American Indian Community Colleges, a list of treaties dealing with Indian education, and a select bibliography. The document is illustrated with a number of photographs.

Torrance, E. Paul. *Discovery and Nurturance of Giftedness in the Culturally Different*. (ED 145-621). Reston, VA: Council for Exceptional Children, 1977. 72 pp.

This monograph presents the author's insights and proposed solutions for the education of gifted, culturally different children.

Tumin, Melvin M. and Plotch, Walter. *Pluralism in a Democratic Society*. New York: Praeger Publishers, 1977. 248 pp.

Presentation of concepts defined at a conference titled, "Pluralism in a Democratic Society," held in New York in 1975, under the sponsorship of the B'nai B'rith Anti-Defamation League and funded by the Ethnic Heritage Studies Program, U.S. Office of Education.

U.S. Commission on Civil Rights. *A Better Chance to Learn: Bilingual Bicultural Education*. Washington, DC: Author, 1975. 250 pp.

This report provides educators and the general public with information about bilingual bicultural education as a means for equalizing educational opportunity for language minority students.

U.S. Commission on Civil Rights. *Sex Bias in the U.S. Code*. (ED 145-307). Washington, DC: Author, 1977. 230 pp.

This report was prepared pursuant to Public Law 85-315, as amended. It is an assessment of the status of women under federal law. It surveys the United States Code identifying sex-based references, discussing possible solutions, and advocating action on the part of Congress and the President in ending the bias which remains in the law.

U.S. Commission on Civil Rights. *Statement on the Equal Rights Amendment*. Washington, DC: Author, 1978. 32 pp.

Ratification of the ERA would for the first time extend to women a clear and full status of equal citizenship under the Constitution. The text of the ERA makes no mention of either sex, and the principle of equality expressed is as much for men as for women.

U.S. Commission on Civil Rights. *Twenty Years after Brown: A Report of the U.S. Commission on Civil Rights*. Washington, DC: Author, 1978. 187 pp.

Details past discrimination including slavery, reconstruction policy, segregation, the civil rights movement and the growth of nonviolent protest. Litigation and equality of educational and economic opportunity and information on equal opportunity in housing are provided. The Brown Decision and letters of transmittal are appended to this volume, as well as numerous charts and tables for reference.

Universal Esperanto Association. *Esperanto Documents*. New Series: No. 1 (1975), No. 2 (1975), No. 3 (1976). Rotterdam, The Netherlands: Universal Esperanto Association.

History and information concerning the international language, Esperanto, and its relationship to world communication.

Urzua, Roberto; Cotera, Martha P.; and Stepp, Emma Gonzalez (eds). *Library Services to Mexican Americans: Policies, Practices, and Prospects*. (ED 151-110). Austin: ERIC-CRESS, National Educational Laboratory Publishers.

New concepts, trends and information in the area of library services for the second largest minority population in the U.S.

Valencia, Atilano A. *Bilingual-Bicultural Education for the Spanish-English Bilingual*. (ED 145-984). Las Vegas, NM: New Mexico Highland University Press, 1972. 83 pp.

Description and rationale for bilingual-bicultural education.

Valencia, Atilano A. (ed). *Selected Readings in Multicultural Education*. Las Vegas, NM: New Mexico Highlands University, Department of Education, 1974. 33 pp.

A collection of essays, some in Spanish, dealing with bilingual and multicultural education, curriculum, and Hispanic folklore.

Von Euler, Mary and Lambers, Gail (eds). *The Catholic Community and the Integration of Public and Catholic Schools*. Washington, DC: National Institute of Education, 1979. 64 pp.

Papers from a conference sponsored by the National Catholic Conference for Interracial Justice in cooperation with the National Catholic Education Association and the Department of Education of the U.S. Catholic Conference, May 1978.

Weinberg, Meyer. *Minority Students: A Research Appraisal*. (ED 137 483). Washington, DC: National Institute of Education, U.S. Department of HEW, 1977. 398 pp.

This volume places research on minority students in a broader framework than is customary. Factors treated at some length include historical and legal background, the ideology of racism, a continuing reexamination and questioning of prevailing views of the role of social class and race in learning, and the impact of minority communities upon the schools. Separate chapters deal with Spanish-surnamed and American Indian students. The impact of schooling is examined in the areas of academic achievement, self-concept and aspirations, and the relationships of students among themselves and with their teachers.

Weinberg, Meyer. *A Chance to Learn: A History of Race and Education in the United States*. Cambridge, MA: Cambridge University Press, 1977. 470 pp.

This book is a history of the educational experience of Black, Mexican American, American Indian, and Puerto Rican children in the U.S. At the heart of the story is the unending attempt of minority parents to assure their children a chance to learn. Wherever possible, these efforts are documented from primary historical sources.

Wenk, Michael; Tomasi, S. M.; and Baroni, Geno (eds). <u>Pieces of a Dream: The Ethnic Worker's Crisis with America</u>. New York: Center for Migration Studies, 1972. 212 pp.

Fifteen essays concerning the ethnic worker's crisis with America. Contributors include Senator Richard Schweiker, Edmund Muskie, Representative Pucinski, former Mayor John Lindsey, former President of the AFL-CIO George Meany, former secretary of Labor Hodgson, and other academic and community organization authors.

Westoff, Leslie Aldridge. <u>Women--In Search of Equality</u>. Focus #6. Princeton, NJ: Educational Testing Service, 1979. 17 pp.

Addresses limiting sex stereotypes, women and government, development across the ages, the math myth, and helping women to find themselves.

Wise, James H. (ed). <u>Proceedings: Conference on Corporal Punishment in the Schools--A National Debate</u>. (ED 144-185). Washington, DC: National Institute of Education, 1977. 61 pp.

This national invitational conference was held February 18-20, 1977. It was hosted by the Child Protection Center of Children's Hospital, National Medical Center, Washington, DC.

Part 3: Directories

Brownson, Charles B. Congressional Staff Directory. Mt. Vernon, VA: Congress Staff Directory (P. O. Box 62, Mt. Vernon, VA 22121).

In its 21st edition, this privately published yearly directory lists all Senate and House office staff and committees by name, location in DC and the home state and telephone. Also included are district numbers in cities and towns, key administrative personnel (i. e. Executive Branch of government) and biographies of Senators and Representatives.

Cole, Katherine W. (ed). Minority Organizations: A National Directory. Garrett Park, MD: Garrett Park Press.

The directory lists 580 Black, 741 Native American, 348 Asian American, 486 Hispanic, and 550 general minority-oriented organizations. Another 545 organizations are cited along with their last address. This directory will be expanded and updated approximately every two years.

Directory: Multicultural Education In U.S. Teacher Education Institutions, 1978. Washington, DC: American Association of Colleges for Teacher Education, 1978.

This directory was compiled from data collected in a "Survey of Multicultural Education in Teacher Education" by AACTE's Commission on Multicultural Education during the fall of 1977. The information included in this directory is based on the responses of the 387 institutions that returned the survey.

Fuchigami, Robert Y. Minority Professional Talent Bank Directory. Reston, VA: The Council for Exceptional Children, 1978. 37 pp.

This directory provides a system for identifying and involving CEC members of minority background in various organizational activities.

Gollnick, Donna M. Profile of the Multicultural/Bilingual Education Activities of Professional and Related Education Organizations. Unpublished document. Washington, DC: American Association of Colleges for Teacher Edcuation, 1978. 75 pp.

The multicultural/bilingual education activities of 32 selected national organizations are described. A bibliography of related documents published by these organizations is included along with the text of related policy statements supportive of multicultural education and/or bilingual education.

Hinds, Charles F. (ed). Concise Catalog of Federal Programs Within Education and Arts Cabinet. Frankfort, KY: Education and Arts Cabinet, State Department of Education, 1977. 165 pp.

The Kentucky compilation of Federal progrms had as its beginning point the National Catalog of Federal Domestic Assistance. The basic financial information was provided by the fiscal officers of the agencies surveyed. The data refers to actual federal expenditures for Fiscal Year 1976 and to anticipated federal expenditures for Fiscal Year 1977. Since there has been so much confusion about actual funds available, the information may be useful to budget officials and agency heads as well as to the General Assembly. It is presented here as a model for educators.

Johnson, Willis L. (ed). Director of Special Programs for Minority Group Members: Career Information Services, Employment Skills Banks, Financial Aid Sources. Garrett Park, MD: The Garrett Park Press. 1975. 400 pp.

A comprehensive listing of special programs for minority group members concerned with upward mobility. The Directory is organized into four sections: general employment and educational assistance programs, federal programs, women's programs, and college and university awards.

National Alliance of Businessmen. Directory of Predominantly Black Colleges and Universities in the United States of America. Washington, DC: National Alliance of Businessmen.

This directory is an effort to establish stronger ties between industry and minority colleges and to provide channels for affirmative action in employment on behalf of graduates of the institutions listed.

National Institute for Education. *A Citizen's Guide to School Desegregation Law.* (ED 160-689). Washington, DC: National Institute of Education, 1978. 55 pp.

   The National Institute of Education prepared these summaries of recent major court decisions related to school desegregation in an effort to be of assistance to non-lawyers.

The National Institute of Education. *School Desegregation: A Report of State and Federal Judicial and Administrative Activity* (ED 146-317). Washington, DC: The National Institute of Education, 1977. 44 pp.

   A list by state of judicial and administrative activities by the states and federal government to enforce school desegregation.

Office of the Federal Register, National Archives and Records Service, General Services Administration. *The Federal Register, What It Is and How To Use It.* Washington, DC: U.S. Government Printing Office, 1978. 100 pp.

   All administrative procedures which result from and relate to federal laws are published in the Federal Register daily editions. Indexes, abstracts, information, location and use are explained.

Turner, William H. and Michael, John A. *Traditionally Black Institutions of Higher Education: Their Identification and Selected Characteristics.* Washington, DC: National Center for Education Statistics, 1978. 10 pp.

   Identifies 106 traditionally Black institutions, describes the procedures used to compile the list, and presents selected items of descriptive information about each institution.

Ulrich's International Periodicals Directory, Eighteenth Edition 1979-1980 (A Bowker Serials Bibliography). New York: R. R. Bowker Co. 2156 pp.

   Classified guide to current domestic and foreign periodicals.

U.S. Commission on Civil Rights. <u>A Guide to Federal Laws and
Regulations Prohibiting Sex Discrimination</u>. Washington, DC:
U.S. Commission on Civil Rights, 1976. 189 pp.

This booklet explains current Federal laws that prohibit sex
discrimination, as well as policies and regulations of
Federal agencies prohibiting sex discrimination. The booklet
describes the major provisions of each law and regulation and
the complaint procedures established under each.

U. S. Congress. <u>Congressional Directory</u>. Washington, DC:
U.S. Government Printing Office.

Data on members of Senate and House listed by state and
district, committee membership, terms of service,
administrative assistant and/or secretary, room, telephone;
officials of courts, military establishments, other federal
departments, D. C. government, governors of states and
territories, foreign diplomats.

Washburn, David E. <u>Ethnic Studies, Bilingual/Bicultural Education
and Multicultural Teacher Education in the United States: A
Directory of Higher Education Programs and Personnel</u>. Miami,
FL: Inquiry International, 1979. 304 pp.

A comprehensive directory of programs and personnel in the
areas of ethnic studies, multicultural teacher education, and
bilingual/bicultural education. This directory is the result
of a survey of the 3,083 postsecondary institutions in the
United States and outlying areas. It was conducted during
the 1977-1978 academic year.

<u>Washington Information Directory</u>. Washington, DC: Congressional
Quarterly.

Sources of information divided into agencies of the executive
branch, Congress, and private or "non-governmental"
organizations; includes name of organization, address,
telephone number, name and title of director and a
description of the work performed by the agency, committee or
organization.

Wynar, Lubomyer R. and Wynar, Anna T. <u>Encyclopedic Director of
Ethnic Newspapers and Periodicals in the United States</u>. 2nd
edition. Littleton, CO: Libraries Unlimited, 1976. 256 pp.

This new updated and completely revised edition of the
directory, appearing in the Bicentennial year, aims primarily
to serve not only scholars engaged in the study of the
American society and ethnic groups but also librarians
involved in reference service and the building of ethnic
collections.

Part 4: Evaluation Guidelines, Reports, and Studies

The American College Testing Program (ACT). *Development and Validation of Sex-Balanced Interest Inventory Scales.* ACT Research Report 78. Iowa City, IA: Author, 1977. 36 pp.

This report describes the development and validation of the Unisex ACT Interest Inventory (UNIACT). In contrast to other interest inventories in common use, the UNIACT contains scales on which males and females receive similar scores.

American Council on Education. *Framework for Evaluating Institutional Commitment to Minorities: A Guide to Institutional Self-Study.* (ED 123-981). Washington, DC: American Council on Education, 1976. 14 p.

The immediate objective of the FRAMEWORK is to promote reassessment of institutional programs and policies that affect minorities. The broader goal is to bring some order, understanding, and renewed energy to practices that influence institutions' commitments to equal educational opportunity for all persons.

American Institutes for Research. *Evaluation of the Impact of ESEA Title VII Spanish/Engish Bilingual Education Program.* Washington, DC: U.S. Office of Education, Office of Planning, Budget and Evaluation, 1977. 189 pp.

These reports are available from the US Office of Education and also through the ERIC System: INTERIM RESULTS - ED 138-100; OVERVIEW OF STUDY - ED 154-634; Vol. 2: PROJECT DESCRIPTION - ED 138-091; Vol. III: YEAR TWO IMPACT DATA, EDUCATIONAL PROCESS, AND IN-DEPT ANALYSES - ED 154-635; Vol. I: STUDY DESIGN and INTERIM FINDINGS - ED 138-090.

Britton, Gwyneth and Lumpkin, Margaret. *A Consumer's Guide to Sex, Race and Career Bias in Public School Textbooks.* Corvallis, OR: Britton and Associates, 1977. 290 pp.

A guide for evaluating textbooks for sex, race, and career bias. Describes the bias now existing in most texts.

Burry, James. Evaluation Report of the Teacher Corps Cycle XII and Program 78 Developmental Training Conference. Los Angeles: Teacher Corps, Center for the Study of Evaluation, University of California, 1978. 115 pp.

Evaluation of the 1978 Teacher Corps National Conference attended by 1,200 individuals. Multicultural education was one of the programmatic strands of this meeting.

Coffin, Gregory C.; Harley, Elsie F.; and Rhodes, Bessie M. L. Black History: A Test to Create Awareness and Arouse Interest. Marblehead, MA: Coffin Associates, 1974. (2 booklets, 17 and 14 pp.)

This test is designed to encourage teachers at all levels to examine their curricula for correcting omissions and distortions. The objective is that teachers will gain the knowledge necessary to help reinforce the self-image of Black children.

Council on Interracial Books for Children. Human and Anti-Human Values in Children's Books. New York, NY: Council on Interracial Books for Children, 1976. 280 pp.

A guide for effective evaluation of children's books, including explanations of terminology and evaluation concepts. A check-list on specific books, through 1975, analyses, author/subject indexes are included.

Daniel, Philip T. K. A Report on the Status of Black Studies Programs in Midwestern Colleges and Universities. DeKalb, IL: Center for Minority Students, Northern Illinois University, 1977. 35 pp.

The primary purpose of this study was to determine the rise or decline of Black Studies Programs in midwestern colleges and universities. The components of existing programs are compared with those that no longer exist. The report also examines critical opinions, related research, and government legislation.

Gallagher, Buell G. (ed). National Association of Colored Peoples: Report on Minority Testing. (ED 128-535). New York: NAACP Special Contribution Fund 1976. 36 pp.

A report of the NAACP Conference on Testing. Calls for a moratorium on all current standardized tests unless such instruments conform to NAACP recommendations. Report of the task force deals with the use and misuse of these tests, the psychometric integrity of the tests, public policy, and fair testing codes. A selected bibliography and list of participants are included.

Hawaii State Instructional Services. *Identification, Assessment & Planning System for Limited English Speakers (IAPS): A Comprehensive Plan.* Hawaii: State Department of Education, 1976. 142 pp.

The purpose of this system is to ensure adequate identification and assessment of the limited-English speaking target group in order that appropriate special services may be provided. It is anticipated that the data collected will be incorporated into the future Pupil Records Module of the Department.

Hilliard, Asa G. *Alternatives to IQ Testing: An Approach to the Identification of Gifted Minority Children.* (ED 146-009). Sacramento: Frederic Burk Foundation for Education, California State Department of Education, Special Education Support Unit, 1976.

An instrument for use in pre-screening and identification of "gifted minority" students has been developed, piloted, and refined as a part of this study. However, a major part of this study is the treatment of the literature, the synthesis of data from interviews with practicing clinicans, and the development of a rationale. The pre-screening instrument is merely a small part of a much larger and more complex process, and is itself more of a guide to observation than a test in the traditional sense.

ISTE Report IV: Creative Authority and Collaboration. Washington, DC: Inservice Teacher Education Concepts Project, Teacher Corps, US Office of Education, 1976. 160 pp.

The Inservice Teacher Education Concepts Project was undertaken jointly by the National Teacher Corps Resource Centers and the National Center for Educational Statistics. The purpose of the reports is to (a) determine data needs, (b) clarify concepts and (c) guide activities. Resources include existing literature and survey of opinion of knowledgeable representative groups and individuals.

Johnson, Syvia T. *The Measurement Mystique: Issues In Selection for Professional Schools and Employment.* Washington, DC: Institute for the Study of Educational Policy, Howard University, 1979. 48 pp.

> A review of the state of the art in testing and measurement as they relate to the admissions process. The author examines measurement for selection, the origins and identification of test bias, using regression analysis in determining predictive validity, and the overprediction issue. A bibliography is included.

Locks, Nancy A.; Pletcher, Barbara A.; and Reynolds, Dorothy F. *Language Assessment Instruments for Limited-English-Speaking Students.* Washington, DC: The National Institute of Education, 1978. 50 pp.

> Provides information on adequacy of available instruments and indicates areas of need. NIE contracted with the American Institutes for Research (AIR) of Palo Alto, California to compile the report as a companion to the *Catalogue of Assessment Instruments for Limited English-Speaking Students, 1977.*

Multicultural Teacher Education: Guidelines Toward Implementation. Washington, DC: American Association of Colleges for Teacher Education, 1980. 27 pp.

> A set of guidelines for planning and evaluating multicultural teacher education programs. These guidelines go beyond the minimum requirements of the NCATE Standards toward designing teacher education programs that reflect a commitment to multicultural education and the provision of educational equity.

National Advisory Committee on Black Higher Education and Black Colleges and Universities. *Reports on Approaches to Higher Education for Black Americans.* Annual Reports for 1977 and 1978; Interim Reports for 1979. Washington, DC: U. S. Department of Health, Education and Welfare.

> Examines access of Black students to higher education, including the Black colleges.

National Assessment of Educational Progress. *Hispanic Student Achievement in Five Learning Areas: 1971-75.* (ED 138-414). Washington, DC: U.S. Government Printing Office, 1977. 65 pp.

National assessment, by regions, in the following curricular areas: science, citizenship, writing, literature, and social studies.

National Council for Accreditation of Teacher Education. <u>Standards for Accreditation of Teacher Education</u>. Washington, DC: Author, 1977. 29 pp.

Standards that must be met by teacher education institutions seeking accreditation or reaccreditation by the National Council for Accreditation of Teacher Education. Both the basic and advanced standards include a standard and other references to multicultural education.

National Education Association. <u>School Desegregation Guidelines for Local and State Education Associations</u>. Washington, DC: Author, 1974. 26 pp.

General principles outlined would be appropriate for education associations to urge upon all school districts facing desegregation. Specific principles are suggested regarding school governance, assignment of education personnel, student rights, and the instructional program. An additional section discusses principles applicable to desegregation of metropolitan or multiple school districts and upon the courts. A selected bibliography is appended, along with a list of resources available to local leaders involved in desegregation.

Newton, James E. <u>A Curriculum Evaluation of Black Studies in Relation to Student Knowledge of Afro-American History and Culture</u>. Saratoga, CA: R&E Research Associates, 1976. 102 pp.

Development and utilization of an assessment measure to provide a description of student knowledge of Afro-American history and culture in relation to Black Studies. Examines the effect Black Studies has upon student knowledge of Afro-Americans and their contributions to the American cultural and social system.

Noar, Gertrude. <u>Human Rights Behaviors of the Teacher: A Self Assessment</u>. Norman, OK: Phi Delta Kappa, Teacher Education Project on Human Rights, University of Oklahoma. 5 pp. (Limited Publication)

Concepts for self-assessment by teachers and assessment of teachers by students; Developed in relation to the Institutional and Individual Human Rights Teacher Behavior Study by the Phi Delta Kappa through the University of Oklahoma.

Orozco, Cecillo. *A Graduate Training Program Developed for Elementary School Spanish-English Bilingual Teachers.* (ED 115-644). Albuquerque: College of Education, University of New Mexico (Sponsored by Title V, ESEA, Office of Education, Department of HEW), 1975. 140 pp.

An evaluation of training needs of prospective bilingual (Spanish/English) elementary school teachers who did not graduate from a bilingual B. A. program. Questionnaires, responses and revisions involving participants, faculty, and directors are described.

Phi Delta Kappa, Teacher Education Project on Human Rights. *An Instrument for the Evaluation of Institutional and Individual Human Rights Behaviors in Teacher Education Institutions.* Norman, OK: University of Oklahoma. 16 pp. (Limited Publication)

Developed by the Phi Delta Kappa National Policy Committee for Human Rights in Teacher Education, this evaluation is addressed to students, teachers and administrators.

Sadker, Myra and Sadker, David. *Beyond Pictures and Pronouns: Sexism in Teacher Education Textbooks.* Washington, DC: U.S. Government Printing Office, 1979. 71 pp.

The findings of this study reveal widespread sex bias in the most popular teacher education textbooks.

Social Science Education Consortium, Inc. *Ethnic Studies Materials Analysis Instrument.* (ED 128-279). Social Science Education Consortium, 1976. 29 pp.

This instrument was designed to aid classroom teachers who are preparing curriculum for ethnic studies by providing them with an instrument for analyzing the educational soundness and ethnic accuracy of materials. It was developed as part of a grant from the Ethnic Heritage Studies Program, U.S. Office of Education, 1974.

Tittle, Carol Kehr. *Sex Bias in Testing: A Review With Policy Recommendations.* (ED 164-623). Princeton, NJ: ERIC Clearinghouse on Tests, Measurement and Evaluation, Educational Testing Service with the Women's Educational Equity Communications Network.

The variety of procedures used in studies indicates that there is not one procedure or definition that will quickly tell the policy maker, test user, or test publisher that an educational test is or is not biased against women. This monograph reflects the state of the art in both testing and analyses related to educational equity.

Weitzman, Lenore J. and Rizzo, Diane. *Biased Textbooks: A Research Perspective. Action Steps You Can Take.* (ED 119-114). Washington, DC: The National Foundation for the Improvement of Education, 1974. 15 pp.

Drawing on their comprehensive research study, the authors describe and analyze stereotyping in elementary texts. Includes suggestions for dealing with biased textbooks.

Williams, Byron; Santos-Rivera, Iris; and Alcala, Consuelo. *Manual for Evaluating Content of Classroom Instructional Materials for Bilingual-Multicultural Education.* (ED 160-276). San Diego: Institute for Cultural Pluralism, San Diego State University.

A collection of resources for evaluating the content of classroom instructional materials for bilingual and multicultural education.

Women on Words and Images. *Dick & Jane as Victims: Sex Stereotyping in Children's Readers.* (ED 065-832). Princeton, NJ: Author, 1975. 80 pp.

A content analysis of the readers published prior to 1972 from fourteen major publishers. Outcomes show the limitations of sex role conditioning. Part II includes information about the readers that have been published since 1972. The results have been disappointing (a series of non-sexist readers has not yet been discovered). Guidelines are provided to enable people involved with children's books to analyze the types of books that are used. Further suggestions regarding classroom activities and a bibliography for further reading are also included.

Women's Educational Equity Act: First Annual Report.
    Washington, DC: Office of Education, 1976. 53 pp. (Second
    Annual Report, 1977; Third Annual Report, 1978; and Fourth
    Annual Report, 1979).

The Women's Educational Equity Act authorizes the support of
an extremely broad range of activities that target on every
area of education that perpetuates sex bias. The First
Annual Report covers the period since the enactment of the
Law on August 21, 1974, to the close of its first fiscal year
of operation, September 30, 1976.

Part 5: Historical References

Almeida, Raymond A. and Nyhan, Patricia. *Cape Verde and Its People: A Short History and Folk Tales of the Cape Verdean People.* Boston, MA: The American Committee for Cape Verde, 1976. 27 pp.

These booklets examine the relationship between Cape Verde and America through history and folk tales.

Bales, Carol Ann. *Tales of the Elders.* Chicago, IL: Follett, 1977. 160 pp.

Stories of men and women who were immigrant settlers in the United States, 1900-1930.

Barrett, Leonard E. *Soul-Force: African Heritage in Afro-American Religion.* New York: Doubleday Anchor, C. Eric Lincoln Series on Black Religion, 1974. 25 pp.

Various religious cults developed by Africans in the New World are examined. Most of the book is based on materials gathered in field research in Africa, the West Indies, and the USA. Bibliography included.

Bogle, Donald. *Toms, Coons, Mulattoes, Mammies, and Bucks: An Interpretive History of Blacks in American Films.* New York: Bantam Books, 1973. 364 pp.

An interpretive history of Blacks in American films.

Buckalwe, L. W. and Wynn, Cordell. *Black American Heritage: Contributions to the American Culture.* Huntsville, AL: Southern Press, 1978. 202 pp. (Limited Publication)

Seventeen essays on Black American heritage relating to aspects and dimensions of psychology, philosophy, literature, history, natural science, physical science, education, and human relations.

Chinweizu, *The West and the Rest of Us: White Predators, Black Slavers and the African Elite.* New York: Random House, Vintage Books, 1975. 520 pp.

A critical investigation into the purposes and styles of western imperialist expansion during the past 500 years.

Cordasco, Francesco (ed). *Studies in Italian American Social History*. Totowa, NJ: Rowman and Littlefield, 1975. 251 pp.

Essays by fifteen authors, compiled in honor of the Italian American historiographer, Leonard Covello (1887-).

Coye, Molly Joel and Livingston, John (eds). *China Yesterday and Today*. New York: Bantam Books, 1975. 458 pp.

This study of China includes Chinese poetry, fiction and such historic documents as Mao Tse-Tung's report on the peasant movement in Hunan province and the U.S. Foreign Service Officer reports of John S. Service and John Paton Davis. Divergent viewpoints come from such eminent China authorities as John D. Fairbanks, Harold Lamb, Owen Lattimore, Edwin O. Reischauer, Edgar Snow, Arthur Waley, and Theodore H. White. Several maps and an annotated bibliography are also included.

Diop, Cheikh Anna. *The African Origin of Civilization: Myth or Reality*. New York: Lawrence Hill and Co., 1974. 317 pp.

Documentation and conclusions based on a historical theory which refutes many ideas previously presented by Egyptian linguists and historians. This volume includes several chapters from the author's first publication (1954) *Black Nations and Culture*. Translated from the French by Mercer Cook.

Downs, Ray F. *Japan Yesterday and Today*. New York: Bantam Books, 1971. 256 pp.

A collection of historical and sociopolitical essays by Western and Oriental authors, arranged in a chronological format.

Erdoes, Richard E. *The Sun Dance People: The Plains Indians, Their Past and Present*. New York: Random House, 1973. 215 pp.

Contemporary prints and photographs provide a visual record of earlier times, while the author's own photographs and descriptive history present the Plains Indians as modern individuals, struggling to save their lands, their way of life, their identity.

Gumina, Deanna Paoli. The Italians of San Francisco 1850-1930. New York: Center for Migration Studies 1978. 230 pp.

A completely bilingual, Italian-English case study, this work is an introduction to further study of the economic and social progress of the Italians in California. It concerns the years from the admission of California to the Union in 1850 to the census of 1930, which acknowledged that the Italians outnumbered all other immigrant groups in the state.

Gunther, Lenworth (ed). Black Image: European Eyewitness Accounts of Afro- American Life. Port Washington, NY: Kennikat Press 1978. 160 pp.

Contains three perspectives: views on Blacks, on American Whites, and on foreign white racial attitudes. Twenty-three selections are included, beginning with Cadamosto's impressions of West African life in the fifteenth century and ending with a description of events in the south in 1967-68, a climactic period in the civil rights struggle.

Haskins, James. The Life and Death of Martin Luther King, Jr.. New York: Lothrop, Lee and Shepard, 1977. 160 pp.

Illustrated by photographs, this biography is written for high school and adult readers. It includes an account of his harassment by the FBI, the role of James Earl Ray, his assassin, and still emerging facts about King's life.

Hecht, Marie B.; Berbrich, Joan D.; Healey, Sally A.; and Cooper, Clare M. The Women, YES! New York: Holt, Rinehart and Winston, 1976. 220 pp.

The history of women in America is presented in terms of documentation, definition and discourse, with biographical sketches and illustrations which are suitable for a textbook in women's studies, or sociology, history at the high school and college levels.

Hodges, Norman E. W. *Breaking the Chains of Bondage*. New York, NY: Simon and Schuster, 1972. 492 pp.

An original historical interpretation of the events of the Black experience from its early origins in Africa to the tumultuous 1970's. No single source in Black historiography has been relied upon in this volume, rather many varying sources, both primary and secondary, were used to provide an interpretive and concise history.

Jackson, Curtis E. and Galli, Marcia J. *A History of the Bureau of Indian Affairs and Its Activities Among Indians*. San Francisco, CA: R and E Research Associates, 1977. 162 pp.

Explores the history of the Bureau of Indian Affairs and the development of its activities. The purpose is to provide Indians and nonIndians with deeper and broader insights about the vast expanse of happenings among Indians and, particularly, about the dealings of the federal government with Indian tribes and their members. These dealings and the resulting BIA activities are spread across the whole life of the nation and had their beginnings in the three centuries preceding the founding of the Republic.

McCunn, Ruthanne Lum. *An Illustrated History of the Chinese in America*. San Francisco, CA: Design Enterprises of San Francisco.

The contributions of the Chinese to the development of America are, for the most part, an untold story. Many of the old photographs in the books are being published for the first time.

Miaso, Jozef. *The History of the Education of Polish Immigrants in the United States*. Warsaw, Poland: Polish Scientific Publishers, 1977. 282 pp.

A synthesis of the history of Polish American education in the United States.

Montalvo, David; Deguera, Alida; Ledee, Marcos; and Sandstrom, Eleanor. *The Puerto Ricans: A Brief Look at their History*. New York: Anti-Defamation League of the B'nai B'rith, 1974. 108 pp.

Historical survey of Puerto Rico and its Spanish-American colonial rule. Includes selected bibliography and A-V resources as well as resource centers.

Murphy, Sharon. Other Voices. Dayton, OH: Black, Chicano, and American Indian Press, 1974. 132 pp.

Covers the history of the major minority media--Blacks, Indians, and Spanish Americans--and points out that both Black-owned and Indian-owned newspapers were being published in the United States in the 1830's. It contains a wealth of examples and quotes from minority news people and personalities, etc., on the problems and promises of their craft.

Ethnic Chronology Series. Dobbs Ferry, NY: Oceana Publications.

This series includes the following books:

> The Arabs in America, 1978.
> The Czechs in America. 1978.
> The American Indian, 1492-1976, 1977.
> The Blacks in America, 1492-1976, 1977.
> The Chicanos in America, 1540-1974, 1977.
> The Russians in America, 1727-1970, 1977.

This continuing series contains 28 different books. Each includes a chronological section, documentary material, a selected bibliography and relevant appendices. Originally, the series was designed for secondary schools, but has since been expanded to college level and general research. Titles before 1977 include chronologies on the following ethnic groups in the U.S.: British, Chinese, Dutch, Estonians, Filipinos, French, Germans, Hungarians, Irish, Italians, Japanese, Jews, Koreans, Latvians, Lithuanians, Poles, Portugese, Puerto Ricans, Romanians, Scandinavians, Spanish, Ukrainians.

Roach, Hildred. Black American Music: Past and Present. Boston: Crescendo Publishing Co., 1973. 199 pp.

An historical survey of Afro American composers and their music, 1619 to 1970. Styles, themes, cultural and historical significance are stressed, including interrelationships between North American and African musical courses. Short, biographical sketches of the composers are presented as well as a glossary, bibliography, and list of recordings.

Schweitzer, Frederick M. *A History of the Jews Since the First Century, A.D.*. New York: Macmillan Co., 1971. 319 pp.

Presents a Christian scholar's objective view of Jewish-Gentile relations in a historical context.

Servin, Manuel P. *An Awakened Minority: The Mexican Americans.* Second edition. Beverly Hills: Glencoe Press, 1974. 309 pp.

Twenty-two previously unpublished historical essays arranged in a chronological sequence, beginning with the Spanish colonial period in California.

Standing Bear, Luther. *My People The Sioux.* Lincoln, NB: University of Nebraska Press, 1975. 288 pp.

The preparation of this book has not been with any idea of self-glory. It is just a message to the white race; to bring my people before their eyes in a true and authentic manner. The American Indian has been written about by hundred of authors of white blood or possibly by an Indian of mixed blood who has spent the greater part of his life away from a reservation. These are not in a position to write accurately about the struggles and disappointments of the Indian. (Preface)

Sterling, Dorothy (ed). *The Trouble They Seen: Black People Tell the Story of Reconstruction.* Garden City, NY: Doubleday, 1976. 480 pp.

A documentary history of the American reconstruction period, 1865-1877, with over 150 illustrations, editorial comments, index.

Part 6: Literature and Art References

Acosta, Oscar Zeta. *The Revolt of the Cockroach People*. New York: Bantam Books, 1974. 281 pp.

A contemporary historical novel about the Chicanos of East Los Angeles, California.

Angelou, Maya. *Gather Together in My Name*. New York: Bantam Books, 1974. 181 pp.

The story of a heroine who knows the meaning of struggle and never loses her pride and dignity.

Barrio, Raymond. *Mexico's Art and Chicano Artists*. Sunnyvale, CA: Ventura Press, 1975. 70 pp.

A comprehensive survey of the history of Mexico's art, and its influence on Chicano artists. Illustrations by the author.

Chin, Frank; Chan, Jeffrey Paul; Inada, Lawson Fusao; and Wong, Shawn Hsu. *Aiiieeee! An Anthology of Asian-American Writers*. Washington, DC: Howard University, 1974. 295 pp.

Included are writings of 14 accomplished Americans of Japanese, Chinese, Filipino descent in the genre of prose, poetry, drama, autobiography, short story, and excerpts from novels.

Chisholm, Shirley. *The Good Fight*. New York: Bantam Books, 1973. 191 pp.

The autobiographical story of Congresswoman Shirley Chisholm, the first Black woman to run for President.

Hausman, Gerald. Illustrated by Sidney Hausman. *Sitting on the Blue-Eyed Bear*. Westport, CT: Lawrence Hill and Co., 1975. 130 pp.

There are poem legends about the creation of earth and man, prose legends about animals and nature, and stories about medicine men and their practices. Each section of the book is introduced by a description of how the legends and myths which follow were handed down and became part of the cultural and religious life of the Navajo people. The book also includes a history of the Navajos and a description of their life today.

Hsu, Kai-yu. *The Chinese Literary Scene: A Writer's Visit to the People's Republic.* New York: Random House, Vintage Books, 1975. 264 pp.

This book was prepared by a man who was born in China, left in 1945, became a scholar of journalism and modern Chinese literature in the United States, and returned to China for a six-month visit in 1973. This collection includes a literary discussion and criticism that show changes in mood before and after the Cultural Revolution. Samples of contemporary writing for the theater and short stories dealing with the Chinese proletarian environment are included. Also includes a section of folk songs, ballads, and narratives.

Katz, Jane B. (ed). *I Am the Fire of Time--The Voices of Native American Women.* New York: E.P. Dutton Co., 1977. 201 pp.

Collection of illustrated stories, poems, and memories of Native American Indian women.

Liu, Wu-Chi and Lo, Irving Yucheng (eds). *Sunflower Splendor: Three Thousand Years of Chinese Poetry.* Garden City, NY: Anchor Books, 1975. 630 pp.

This is an anthology of Chinese poetry from the 12th Century, B.C. through the mid-twentieth and Mao Tse-Tung. Over one hundred poets are represented; most of these selections have been translated, or retranslated, specifically for this publication by various East Asian scholars in American and Canada.

MacCracken, Mary. *A Circle of Children.* New York: Signet Books, New American Library, 1975. 218 pp.

Autobiographical story of a teacher's love and dedication to her emotionally disturbed pupils.

National Dissemination and Assessment Center for Bilingual Education (Title VII). *Discovering Folklore through Community Resources.* Austin: National Dissemination and Assessment Center for Bilingual Education, 1979.

A potpourri of Mexican American folklore developed in order to rediscover and preserve a part of the culture of the Mexican Americans including creencias, costumbres, curanderos, cuentos--tidbits of legend and lore.

Nicholas, A. X. The Poetry of Soul. New York: Bantam Books, 1971. 103 pp.

Black poet A. X. Nicholas presents Black songs as poems descended from a long and rich tradition, reflecting the general mood of the Black community toward self-pride and self-determination.

Platt, Kin. The Doomsday Gang. New York: William Morrow and Co., Greenwillow Books, 1978. 185 pp.

The painful story of a boy's search for meaning and self-respect in a world that offers none--and of young lives, honed on the keen edge of violence, hurtling blindly toward doomsday.

Plotz, Helen (ed). As I Walked Out One Evening: A Book of Ballads. New York: Greenwillow Books, William Morrow and Company, Inc. 1976, 288 pp.

Over 130 ballads of the English speaking world with recognizable rhythm, selected for secondary school literature curriculum. Subjects include love, magic, narrative, satire, war, work and love.

Robinson, William H. (ed). NOMMO: An Anthology of Modern Black African and Black American Literature. New York: MacMillan and Co., 1972. 494 pp.

Compiled especially for courses in Black literature, this anthology is centered around the Pan Black Movement, including all cultures with roots in Black Africa. Includes essays, stories, poems, and plays.

Rosen, Kenneth (ed). The Man to Send Rainclouds. New York: Vintage Books, 1975. 178 pp.

Twenty contemporary short stories about Native American folklore, some by young Native Americans. Includes black and white illustrations. Suitable for high school and adult.

Schwarz-Bart, Andre. *A Woman Named Solitude*. New York: Bantam Books, 1974. 145 pp.

A historical novel describing American slavery at the turn of the 19th century.

Time to Greez! Incantations from the Third World. San Francisco: Glide Publications/Third World Publications, 1975. 210 pp.

Over 90 contributions of poetry, prose, and graphics. Introduction by Maya Angelou.

Trambley, Estela Portillo. *Rain of Scorpions and Other Writings*. Berkeley, CA: Tonatiuh International, 1975. 178 pp.

Ten short stories by a contemporary Chicano woman.

Villasenor, Edmund. *Macho!* New York: Bantam Books, 1973. 245 pp.

A contemporary Chicano historical novel.

Washington, William D. and Beckoff, Samuel. *Black Literature: An Anthology of Outstanding Black Writers*. New York: Simon and Schuster, 1972. 316 pp.

Includes poems, plays, novels, letters, folk tales, articles, autobigraphies, and short stories as well as a glossary of terms and suggestions for further reading.

Part 7: Models, Guides, Textbooks, and Activities

Ahlum, Carol and Fralley, Jacqueline. High School Feminist Studies. (ED 135-676). Old Westbury, NY: The Feminist Press, 1976. 153 pp.

Provides an alternative curriculum with several distinctive goals, including (1) to raise the consciousness of students about the sexist curriculum and the wider society; (2) to compensate for the omission of women from the curriculum; (3) to develop the knowledge--through research--necessary to broaden the curriculum; and (4) to recover the lost or neglected history and culture of women of all classes, races, and nationalities.

The American Revolution: Selections from Secondary School History Books of Other Nations. Washington, DC: U. S. Government Printing Office, 1976.

Includes a set of selections from the history texts of 13 nations. It is an effort by educators to gather the curricular perceptions of other countries about key events or periods in American history.

Asian American Bilingual Education Center. Bilingual Curricular Materials, Asian-Pacific Languages and English. Berkeley: Title VII Asian American Bilingual Center, 1979.

A series of curricular guides, elementary to early secondary, including resources for bilingual teachers in Chinese and Filipino. Booklets vary up to 85 pages. Include conceptual monographs in English, e.g., "What Is Filipino?" and "Asian-American Perspectives on Education." Materials are illustrated, and inexpensive. Supply lists and catalogues are available.

Baptiste, H. Prentice, Jr. and Baptiste, Mira Lanier. Developing the Multicultural Process in Classroom Instruction: Competencies for Teachers. Washington, DC: University Press of America, 1979. 245 pp.

Focuses on generic competencies required for acquisition of basic skills and strategies for multiculturalizing curriculum and classroom instruction. It contains competencies, rationales, instructional objectives, enabling activities, and assessment procedures. Its format lends itself to teacher training courses and inservice programs for school districts.

Beckum, Leonard D.; Taylor, Alvin Leon; Chow, Stanley H. L.; Banks, Henry A.; and Uribe, Oscar J., Jr. <u>Technical Assistance: A Guide for Planning, Delivering, and Evaluating Services to School Districts</u>. San Francisco: STRIDE, Far West Laboratory for Educational Research and Development, 1976.

Outlines the procedures used by STRIDE to plan, deliver, and evaluate technical assistance services to school districts. STRIDE is a General Assistance Center funded by the U.S. Office of Education under Title IV of the 1964 Civil Rights Act.

<u>Black in White America: Historical Perspectives</u>, Volumes I, II, III, IV, Teachers' edition for each volume. (ED 068-380; ED 068-381; ED 068-382; and ED 132-076). New York: Macmillan and Co., 1974. 268 pp.

Junior high and high school level history, beginning with Africa in the 17th century, before the invasion of the slave traders. Case study of the Ibo (West Africa) tribal organization; comment by Alex Haley regarding his research for the book <u>Roots</u>. Photographic illustrations. Later issues of this volume deal with the "Search for Unity and Equality" and "The Struggle for Black Identity and Power." Includes personal narratives, poems, music, and portraits of Black teenagers.

Black Studies Program. <u>Curriculum Designs and Methods in Black Studies Development of Cross-Cultural and Interdisciplinary Course Models</u>. (ED 125-509) Pullman, WA: Black Studies Program, Washington State University, 1976. 182 pp.

Report of a summer workshop, funded by HEW in 1975, for Black Studies Program directors in the Pacific Northwest. Included are descriptions of the participants' projects and responses. Includes a bibliography for curriculum development, evaluation tools, and notes on academic perspectives for Black Studies.

Butler, Katie B. <u>Walking in Navajo Footprints</u>. Houston: Multicultural Program, College of Education, University of Houston, 1974. 35 pp.

Elementary (K-3) classroom curriculum module to indicate Navajo life and customs in mid-20th century.

Buu, Tri; Logan, Louisette; and Gordon, Fannetta N. <u>Han Hanh Duoc Gap (Happy) to Meet You)</u>. Harrisburg, PA: Division of Communications, Bureau of Curriculum Services, Pennsylvania Department of Education, 1976. 14 pp.

Brief and simple guideline and general information for the American teacher of newly arrived students from Vietnam.

Canadian Ministry of Education. <u>English as a Second Language/Dialect</u>. Ontario, Canada: Author, 1977. 28 pp.

A curriculum guideline for teachers of English as a second language in the intermediate and senior divisions in Canadian educational system.

Carkhuff, Robert R. and Pierce, Richard. <u>Teacher as Person</u>. Washington, DC: National Education Association and Human Resource Development Press, 1976. 64 pp.

Application of interpersonal communication skills in the classroom and methods of teaching these skills. The stories of Johnny, Susan, and Roger represent the authors' day-to-day experiences with thousands of children who are reaching out to expand their lives through positive growth experiences. Designed to assist NEA members in combating racism and sexism in the schools.

Casteel, J. Doyle; Hallman, Clemens L.; and Trueblood, Felicity M. <u>Cross-Cultural Models of Teaching: Latin American Examples</u>. Gainesville, FL: Center for Latin American Studies, University of Florida, 1976. 161 pp.

Exercises and activities designed to take students and teachers into real life situations. Includes values clarification and concept development activities.

Cole, Ann; Haas, Carolyn; Heller, Elizabeth; and Weinberger, Betty. <u>Children Are Children Are Children</u>. Boston: Little, Brown and Co., 1978. 212 pp.

Descriptions of activities for classroom, recreational settings, and/or the home. Based on cultural traditions and customs of Brazil, France, Iran, Japan, Nigeria, and the Soviet Union. The countries were selected for geographical and ethnic diversity. Age limits are flexible.

Cortes, Carlos E. *Understanding You and Them: Tips for Teaching about Ethnicity*. (ED 120-032). Boulder, CO: Social Science Education Consortium, 1976. 14 pp.

Monograph about ethnicity in the curriculum. Includes teaching activities for ethnic studies, and identifying and evaluating materials and resources.

Earhart, Connie. *Multi-Ethnic Approach to Teaching*. (ED 115-612). Columbia, MO: Midwest Center for Equal Educational Opportunity, University of Missouri, 1975. 22 pp.

Curriculum guide developed in conjunction with the Midwest Center for Equal Educational Opportunity's bibliography of multiethnic materials.

Ferguson, Henry. *Manual for Multicultural and Ethnic Studies*. LaGrange Park, IL: Intercultural Network. 135 pp.

Discussion of the philosophical and educational foundations of cultural learning is followed by a how-to guide for faculty training, curriculum development and program evaluation. Includes 37 lessons for classroom use and practical instructions for developing and publishing one's own teaching materials.

Fersh, Seymour. *ASIA: Teaching About/Learning From*. New York: Teachers College Press, 1978. 180 pp.

The major objective of this book is to consider how Asian studies can contribute to the appropriate kinds of education needed by today's students.

Franco, John M. et al. *Afro-American Contributors to American Life*. Westchester, IL: Benefic Press, 1974. 192 pp.

A social studies text in biographical format, approximately seventh grade level. Developed with the collaboration of the City School District of Rochester, NY.

Gage, Alfred (ed). To Live in Two Worlds: A Handbook for Oklahoma School Administrators on Implementing Bilingual Education Programs. Oklahoma State Department of Education, 1977. 32 pp.

Designed to give the Oklahoma school administrator some basic understanding of bilingual education.

Golden, Edna T. (ed). Learning about the World: Teaching International Studies. Columbus, OH: Ohio State Department of Education, 1976.

Developed for teachers in grades five through eight in order to provide students with information relating to the most basic concepts ingrained in every culture. Background information has been included to help the teacher formulate instructional concepts. Suggested teaching/learning application lessons serve as a guide for teaching the stated concepts. Follow-up activities have been suggested with the hope that students and teachers will generate their own original ideas.

Gollnick, Donna M.; Osayande, Kobla I. M.; and Levy, Jack. Multicultural Teacher Education: Case Studies of Thirteen Programs, Volume II. Washington, DC: AACTE, 1980.

A collection of case studies based on data from site visits to 13 institutions that varied in size, geographical region, and ethnic and racial composition of the student and community populations. The collection presents alternative strategies for implementing multicultural teacher education.

Gorena, Minerva (comp). Information and Materials to Teach the Cultural Heritage of the Mexican-American Child, Grades K-9. Revised version. Austin, TX: Dissemination and Assessment Center for Bilingual Education, 1977. 260 pp.

Includes materials and activity units. Content is organized according to history and overview of Mexico--places to see, celebrations, arts, food, poetry, songs, games, dances, legends, fables and stories, chronology, vocabulary, and bibliography.

Grabowski, John J.; Zak, Judith Zielinski; Boberg, Alice; and Wroblewski, Ralph. Polish Americans and their Communities of Cleveland. Cleveland, OH: Cleveland Ethnic Heritage Studies, Cleveland State University, 1976. 229 pp.

A cultural community case study involving the largest ethnic minority in Cleveland,. As a curriculum demonstration, this study is applicable for college students in the behavioral sciences.

Grant, Gloria (ed). In Praise of Diversity: Multicultural Classroom Applications. Omaha, NE: Teacher Corps, Center for Urban Education, The University of Nebraska at Omaha, 1977. 165 pp.

Written for the classroom teacher interested in implementing multicultural education. The book includes 51 activities written in the following subject areas: social studies, language arts, science/math, and art.

Hansen-Krening, Nancy. Competency and Creativity in Language Arts: A Multiethnic Focus. Reading, MA: Addison-Wesley, 1979. 230 pp.

A resource text for teachers and prospective teachers interested in using multiethnic materials in teaching basic language arts skills, this book may be used either as a supplement to basic texts or as a rationale for both the arts presented and their practical application in the form of model lessons.

Hawaii Bilingual/Bicultural Education Project. The Hawaii Bilingual/Bicultural Education Project: Operational Guidelines, 1977-78. Honolulu: Hawaii State Department of Education, 1977, 35 pp.

These guidelines are consistent with the Department's approved project and proposal and federal regulations for Title VII Bilingual/Bicultural Education. This set of guidelines is a revision of an earlier version distributed in September, 1976.

Hernandez, Elida (ed). Bilingual Education K-3 Resource Manual. Austin, TX: Division of Bilingual Education, Texas Education Agency, 1977. 309 pp.

Prepared as a service to classroom teachers in bilingual education programs, grades K-3. Readings on each of the main instructional areas that make up a balanced state approved program have been included.

Hill, Barbara T. and Oliver, Thomas S. *Multicultural Education: A Modular Approach*. Washington, DC: Division of Teacher Education, University of the District of Columbia, 1977. 100 pp. (Funded by National Teacher Corps.)

Developed through collaboration with four Washington, DC school teachers and clinical interns. The project was undertaken largely due to the prevalence of misinformation and stereotypes about ethnic minorities in urban communities.

Holt International Children's Service. *Tips on the Care and Adjustment of Vietnamese and other Asian Children in the USA*. (ED 116-821). Washington, DC: Children's Bureau, Office of Child Development, U.S. Department of HEW., 1975. 14 pp.

A guide for adoptive parents and teachers of Asian children. Information on culture, food, health, medical requirements for immigrants, psychological hints, e.g., "adjustment shock," and some common words in the native language.

Howard, Suzanne. *Liberating Our Children, Ourselves*. Washington, DC: American Association of University Women, 1975. 60 pp.

A handbook of women's studies course materials for teacher educators, compiled from course materials of more than 50 pioneer women's studies courses in colleges and departments of education.

Illinois Office of Education, Urban and Ethnic Education Section. *Integrating Black Studies into Existing Social Studies Curriculum: A Model Unit*. Chicago, IL: Author, 1975. 90 pp.

This curriculum guide is designed for Black Studies as a part of the larger picture of a curricular approach to cultural pluralism. It is assumed that in the scheme of things, the word "black" could be erased from the title and, in its place, the name of any other ethnic/racial group could be inserted and the aim of this guide would not be altered, save some of the content. It is the process that is important for teachers to follow. (Preface)

Japanese American Citizens League. *The Experiences of Japanese Americans in the United States: A Teacher Resource Manual*. (ED 115-703). San Francisco, CA: Author, 1974. 186 pp.

Includes sections on the history and contemporary concerns of Japanese Americans, suggested instructional activities for grades K-12, and an annotated bibliography of multimedia teacher and student resources.

Jefferson, Margo and Skinner, Elliot P. <u>Roots of Time: A Portrait of African Life and Culture.</u> New York: Zenith Books, 1974. 128 pp.

African societies are contrasted and discussed within the framework of their traditional and contemporary kinship, marriage, religion, and political patterns. Written at junior high to high school level.

Kovac, Roberta; Schwier, Richard; and Stein, Elaine (eds). <u>Kaleidoscope: Activities, Ideas and Sources for Multicultural Education.</u> Bloomington, IN: Lab for Educational Development, School of Education, Indiana University, 1974. 237 pp.

Selected games, recipes, art and craft projects, A-V, books, and periodicals for the elementary level. Includes an evaluation checklist, bibliography, publishers, and resource address.

Lamy, Steven L. <u>Teaching about Ethnic Conflict: Global Issues.</u> Denver, CO: Center for Teaching International Relations, 1978. 110 pp.

Contains all teacher instructions and masters of student materials necessary for classroom use, plus a game titled "Copying."

Lawson, John D.; Griffin, Leslie J.; and Donant, Franklyn D. <u>Leadership Is Everybody's Business: A Practical Guide for Volunteer Membership Groups.</u> San Luis Obispo, CA: Impact Publishers 1976. 221 pp.

Meant to help anyone who, as a member of an organization, has been involved in a directionless discussion, a flakey decision, a meaningless project, or an ambiguous position of leadership.

Lynch, Robert and Smith, Mona. <u>Guidebook: In-Camp Education for Migrant Farmworkers.</u> (ED 143-493). Geneseo, NY: Geneseo Migrant Center, State University College of Arts and Science, 1977. 172 pp.

Presented to motivate those who seek effective means for reaching this mobile population. The suggestions are based upon the Geneseo Migrant Center's experiences with Algonquin Indian, Black, Caucasian, Mexican American, and Puerto Rican migrant workers.

McCune, Shirley and Matthews, Martha (eds). <u>Implementing Title IX and Attaining Sex Equity: A Workshop Package for Postsecondary Educators</u>. Washington, DC: U.S. Government Printing Office, 1978. 150 pp.

Comprises one component of a multicomponent workshop package developed by the Resource Center on Sex Roles in Education under a subcontract with the Council of Chief State School Officers (CCSSO). Includes lectures and activity sheets.

McNamara, Donna B.; Scherer, Joseph J.; and Safferston, Mark J. <u>Preparing for Affirmative Action: A Manual for Practical Training</u>. Includes Leader's Manual. Garret Park, MD: Garret Park Press, 1978.

Originally developed for a two-day workshop to increase one's flexibility to aid in workshop planning. An annotated listing of all exercises is provided. The leader's manual provides guidelines for workshop preparation, directions for exercising leadership, answer sheets, and additional background information.

McNeill, Earldene; Allen, Judy; and Schmidt, Velma. <u>Cultural Awareness for Young Children</u>. The Learning Tree, 1975. 242 pp.

Suggested activities for the preschool classroom or home, including pictures, photos, recipes, bibliographies. Topics include cowboy culture, and Black, Eskimo, Mexican, Native American, Japanese, and Chinese heritage.

Michigan Ethnic Heritage Studies Center. <u>Educational Resources for Ethnic Studies</u>. Detroit: Author, 1977. 103 pp.

An extensive series of ethnic studies material, K-12, adult and college. The project is funded under Title IX, ESEA, in cooperation with public schools and colleges in the southern Michigan area. Study guides, curriculum materials, resource information, bibliographies, and audio-visual materials are included, indexed, and illustrated.

Minneapolis Multiethnic Curriculum Project. Minneapolis, MN: Ethnic Cultural Center, Minneapolis Schools, 1976.

Funded under Title IX of the Elementary and Secondary Education Act, the project has produced curricular units with supplementary materials. The focus is on concepts; examples are subgroups.

Momaday, N. Scott. More than Bows and Arrows: A Study Guide. Seattle: Cinema Associates, 1978. 18 pp.

Description and curriculum application of the film, More than Bows and Arrows, showing the historical impact of Native Americans in the U.S. The film received the 1978 CINE Golden Eagle award by the Committee for International Non-Theatrical Events. Includes a bibliography.

Moore, Robert B. Two History Texts: A Study in Contrasts. (ED 164-209). New York: The Racism and Sexism Resource Center for Educators. 21 pp.

Comparison of two secondary level history textbooks about Mississippi. Comparison of content, format, and illustrations is a part of this high school course in history.

National Association for Women Deans, Administrators, and Counselors. A Grievance Handbook for Women Educators. Washington, DC: 1977. 32 pp.

Designed to serve as a reference and guide for the educator who has an employment related grievance. The primary purpose of the book is to anticipate and answer questions about why, when, where and how to file a grievance.

National Indian Education Association. Contemporary Issues of the American Indian. (ED 103-137). Minneapolis: Author. 50 pp.

The National Indian Education Association, concerned about the proliferation of Indian Studies courses and programs in the colleges and universities attended by American Indian students, in cooperation with the Navajo Community College, conducted extensive research and consultations during 1974 to prepare this model course. The course is designed to provide a competent guide for persons wishing to teach or develop courses in the contemporary subject of American Indians. Bibliographic and source material are included in this model.

National Indochinese Clearinghouse. Indochinese Refugee Education Guides. Arlington, VA: Author, 1976. 31 pp.

This series of guides include topics such as academic resources for teachers of Indochinese students and a bibliography of dictionaries.

National Indochinese Clearinghouse. A Manual for Indochinese Refugee Education (ED 135-236). Washington, DC: National Education Association, 1976.

This packet can be helpful to affiliates of the NEA and to the teachers working with Indochinese refugee children.

Otero, George G. Teaching about Perception: The Arabs. (ED 138-488). Denver, CO: Center for Teaching International Relations, University of Denver, 1977. 92 pp.

This is the first volume in the Cultural Studies Series developed by the University of Denver Graduate School of International Studies. This college-level curriculum focuses on student images of Arabs. Seventeen different activities, plus resources and bibliographies, are included.

Park, Jeanne S. Education in Action: 50 Ideas that Work. Washington, DC: U. S. Government Printing Office, 1978. 128 pp.

Contains 50 short stories describing successful education programs developed and operated with initial funding from the U. S. Office of Education. Each program has been judged under rigorous standards by the Joint Dissemination Review Panel of the Education Division of the Department of Health, Education, and Welfare. Each has been certified "effective" for use by other school districts.

Pasternak, Michael G. Helping Kids Learn Multi-Cultural Concepts: A Handbook of Strategies. Nashville: Teacher Corps, 1977. 249 pp.

Describes the efforts of an urban school system, working in partnership with three universities and community personnel, to create a different kind of school environment--a school environment in which people recognize, accept, and seek to develop the uniqueness of each individual. Provides a wide selection of activities that teachers can use in classrooms. It also delineates the leadership roles teacher educators can assume in a multicultural education training program.

Project PAIUTE. Thus the Old Ones Have Taught Native Americans: A Commentary and Guide for Teachers. (ED 162 771). Reno: Research & Educational Planning Center, College of Education, 1976. 54 pp.

It is the purpose of this guide and commentary to create understanding and to offer some alternatives. This volume is addressed particularly to the non-Indian teacher and the teacher-in-training in order to instill awareness of the child's perspective and to provide direction for teaching about Native American history, art, literature and governance. Some bibliographical and reference materials are also included.

Samora, Julian and Simon, Patricia Vandel. A History of the Mexican-American People. Notre Dame, IN: University of Notre Dame Press, 1977, 238 pp.

Designed to correct the perspective and fill the gap regarding Mexican American history that exists in many American textbooks.

Smith, Gary R. and Otero, George G. Teaching About Cultural Awareness. Denver: Center for Teaching International Relations, University of Denver, 1977, 235 pp.

This book consists of three interrelated sections about cultural awareness. Each section is composed of lessons which can be plugged in or left out of a section or unit, depending on the students' needs and their levels of cultural awareness.

Spencer, Maria Gutierrez and Almance, Sofia. Oayudele! (Help Him/Her.) Santa Fe, NM: Cross Cultural Education Unit, New Mexico Department of Education. 44 pp.

Suggestions to parents and relatives of young children, presented simply and clearly in both English and Spanish. These originated from both parents and teachers in Santa Fe, New Mexico.

Sprung, Barbara. <u>SRA Helps You to Handle Stereotyping.</u> Palo Alto: Research Associates, 1976.

    Reprint in the form of selected monographs from Barbara Spring's <u>Non-sexist Education for Young Children</u>, (1975 - Women's Action Alliance). Focuses primarily on classroom activities and communication.

Student National Education Association. <u>Human Relations Training for Teachers.</u> Washington, DC: Author, 1976. 107 pp.

    This packet is designed to assist state Student NEA affiliates in supporting human relations training as part of a state's teacher certification requirements. It focuses on the regulations and the various ways that five states -- California, Iowa, Oregon, Minnesota, and Wisconsin--went about it. Additional suggestions and materials are also included.

<u>A Study of the State of Bilingual Materials Development and the Transition of Materials to the Classroom.</u> Washington, DC: Office of Evaluation and Dissemination, U.S. Office of Education.

    This study was conducted to determine the availability of bilingual education materials and the extent to which ESEA Title VII projects have improved the current system for producing and marketing materials.

Taylor, Alvin Leon. <u>Workshops: The Educator's Manual for Coordinating the Complete Conference.</u> San Francisco, CA: STRIDE, Far West Laboratory, 1976. 19 pp.

    In response to the numerous requests received for assistance in the development of inservice training sessions, STRIDE presents this manual to assist educators in the coordination of their conferences.

Tiedt, Pamela L. and Tiedt, Iris M. <u>Multicultural Teaching: A Handbook of Activities, Information, and Resources.</u> Boston: Allyn and Bacon, 1979. 353 pp.

    Includes teaching strategies, over 400 classroom activities, and hundreds of sources of commercial and free materials for creating multicultural awareness. This book offers ideas that enable any classroom teacher to promote understanding in the classroom through varied learning experiences focusing on language and culture. Emphasis is placed on developing understandings about ethnic groups within the U.S.

Valverde, Leonard A. (ed). <u>Bilingual Education for Latinos (Education Bilingual Para Latinos)</u>. Washington, DC: Association for Supervision and Curriculum Development, 1978, 120 pp.

A textbook which provides valid guidelines and models to be followed in meeting the challenge of educating the second largest and fastest growing minority population in the United States. Provides a comprehensive theoretical understanding of bilingual education and practical information about program implementation.

Wagen, Robert (ed). <u>Some Essential Learner Outcomes in Social Studies.</u> (ED 146 078). Minneapolis: Division of Instruction, Minnesota Department of Education, 1977, 65 pp.

The goal for this section of K-12 Social Studies Program Renewal is to identify, clarify, seek agreement and commitment to some social studies student outcomes (ends) in the knowledge, skill and attitudes areas around which we can structure social studies content (means) and develop learning activities for students.

Weibust, Patricia S. <u>Learning About the Peoples of Connecticut.</u> Includes a Teacher's Manual. Storrs, CT: University of Connecticut. (Limited Publication)

The Peoples of Connecticut Multicultural Ethnic Heritage Studies are a series of informational books and kits designed to provide basic data and illustrative material about ethnic groups in Connecticut: Irish, Italians, Jews, Puerto Ricans, Armenians, Poles, and Blacks.

Women's Studies Program. <u>In Search of Our Past: Six Units in Women's History</u>. Berkeley, CA: Berkeley Unified School District, Women's Studies Program, 1977-78.

Six curricular units exploring female roles in historical contexts: 1) Native American Women, 2) Southern Women, 3) Women in Struggle, 4) Women in Feudalism, 5) Women in Change, 6) Women and the Industrial Revolution

Wood, Dean D. *Multicultural Canada: A Teachers' Guide to Ethnic Studies.* Toronto, Ontario: The Ontario Institute for Studies in Education, 1978. 138 pp.

A guide to assist teachers in the process of including multiculturalism in social studies curricula. Includes five units of curriculum and instruction in ethnic studies and a selected bibliography of instructional materials.

Part 8: Research Studies

Anderson, Grace M. and Higgs, David. <u>A Future to Inherit: Portuguese Communities in Canada</u>. Ontario, Canada: McClelland and Steward in collaboration with the Secretary of State of Canada, 1976. 200 pp.

Case study of a group of cultural/ethnic communities in Canada. This text is suitable as an example of case study research as well as a resource for curriculum development.

Baker, William P. and Jensen, Henry C. <u>Mexican American, Black and other Graduates and Dropouts: A Follow-up Study Covering 20 Years of Change, 1956-1976</u>. (ED 152-924). San Jose, CA: East Side Union High School District, 1978. 68 pp.

Fifth in a series of follow-up studies of school leavers of the East Side Union High School District.

Brooks, Dennis and Singh, Karamjit. <u>Aspirations Versus Opportunities: Asian and White School Leavers in the Midlands</u>. Leicester, England: Walsall Council for Community Relations in conjuntion with the Commission for Racial Equality. 88 pp.

This study was conceived as a fact finding exercise. It focused on the situation of Black school leavers, girl school leavers, and the combination of these two groups. Its setting was the deteriorating employment situation for school leavers nationally, which was in evidence in 1975 in England.

Cross, William E., Jr. <u>Third Conference on Empirical Research in Black Psychology</u>. Washington, DC: National Institute of Education, 1977. 150 pp.

Reports from the Third Annual Conference on Empirical Reseach in Black Psychology held at Cornell University, October 1976.

Gollnick, Donna M. <u>Multicultural Teacher Education: State of the Scene</u>. Unpublished document. Washington, DC: American Association of Colleges for Teacher Education, 1978.

During the academic year of 1977-78, AACTE collected data from 387 of its 786 institutional members concerning how multicultural education was being developed and implemented within the teacher education program. Beginning in 1979, institutions applying for accreditation or reaccreditation from the National Council for the Accreditation of Teacher Education (NCATE) are required by the recently revised standards to include multicultural education as an integral part of their curriculum design.

Hall, Ron (coordinator). *Proposed Research Plan for Bilingual Education*. Unpublished document. Washington, DC: U.S. Office of Education, 1979. 60 pp.

Plans for Title VII-funded research in bilingual education through 1983.

Howard, Suzanne. *But We Will Persist: A Comparative Research Report on the Status of Women in Academe*. Washington, DC: American Association of University Women, 1978.

Report on the results of a national survey of 588, or 61 percent, of A.A.U.W. affiliates. The study was conducted in 1976 and covered the period of 1973 to 1976. Dr. Howard's research replicates and expands on an earlier survey by Ruth Oltman.

Hunter, William A. *Educational Systems in South Vietnam and of Southeast Asians in Comparison with Educational Systems in the United States*. (ED 155-099). Ames, IA: Research Institute for Studies in Education, Iowa State University, 1977. 279 pp. (Limited Publication)

Describes the educational systems through which Vietnamese and Southeast Asians have come. Also describes the educational systems of Asian countries as they relate to the educational system of the United States.

Kuvlesky, William P. and Boykin, William C. (eds). *Black Youth in the Rural South: Educational Abilities and Ambitions*. Austin, TX: ERIC-CRESS, National Educational Laboratory Publishers, 1979. 89 pp.

The compilation of this review and synthesis is premised upon three considerations: (1) Black youth in the rural south have enough cultural similarities to constitute study as a group; (2) there is an extreme scarcity of consistent and systematic studies of these youth; (3) certain myths concerning Black youth need to be examined under the light of careful scientific research.

Lincoln, Eugene A. White Teachers, Black Schools, and the Inner City: Some Impressions and Concerns. (ED 118-659). Pittsburgh: Division of Teacher Development, University of Pittsburgh, 1975. 85 pp.

A survey-interview study involving 44 white teachers and 28 Black teachers as well as 14 white and 14 Black parents. Questionnaire and responses are given, without statistical analysis. Included is a brief position paper by five educators from the firing line, and a brief bibliography.

National Advisory Committee on Blacks in Higher Education and Black Colleges and Universities. Higher Education Equity: The Crisis of Appearance versus Reality. Washington, DC: U.S. Office of Education, 1978. 68 pp. (Limited Publication)

Review and analysis of available data on Blacks in higher education to determine what tasks must be accomplished and the policies that should be developed by the government and educational entities in order to allow Blacks fuller participation in higher education.

The National Institute of Education. Compensatory Education Study: A Final Report from the National Institute of Education. Washington, DC: Author, 1978. 90 pp.

This volume presents the final report of the study of compensatory education requested by Congress in the 1974 Elementary and Secondary Education Amendments.

Sotomayor, Frank. Para Los Ninos--For the Children. Washington, DC: U.S. Commission on Civil Rights. 28 pp.

A compilation of published and unpublished findings of the Mexican American Education Study, conducted by the U.S. Commission on Civil Rights between 1969 and 1974. Also included is additional information obtained by the writer in interviews with students, parents and educators. The four original reports available are Ethnic Isolation of Mexican Americans, The Unfinished Education, The Excluded Student, Teachers and Students--Differences in Teacher Interaction, and Toward Quality Education.

Standley, Nancy V. White Students Enrolled in Black Colleges and Universities: Their Attitudes and Perceptions. (Ed 165-591). Atlanta, GA: Southern Regiional Education Board, 1978. 43 pp.

This study examines the attitudes and perception white students have of the Black public institutions which they attend, and presents implications to be considered by all of those responsible for public higher education.

Section II

PERIODICAL RESOURCES

Part 1: Journals and Newsletters

AFFIRMATIVE ACTION REGISTER
 (Monthly)
Affirmative Action, Inc.
(For Effective Equal
 Opportunity in Recruitment)
8356 Olive Blvd.
St. Louis, MO 63132
(314) 991-1335
Warren H. Green (ed)
Note: This publication
 maintains listings of
 available positions and
 eligible applicants. Yearly
 subscription--$15.00;
 six-months--$8.00.

AGENDA
Communications Center of the
 National Council of LaRaza
1721 Eye St., N.W. Suite 210
Washington, DC 20006
(202) 659-1251
Miguel Mendiville (ed)

AKWESASNE NOTES (Newsletter)
Program in American Studies of
 the State University of New
 York at Buffalo and D-Q
 University (Davis,
 California)
Mohawk Nation
Rooseveltown, NY 13683
(518) 358-9531
Note: Published five times
 annually (March, May, July,
 September, and December)

AMERICAN HUNGARIAN EDUCATOR
 (Newsletter)
American Hungarian Educators'
 Association
P.O. Box 4103
Silver Spring, MD 20904

AMERICAN INDIAN CULTURE AND
 RESEARCH JOURNAL
American Indian Culture Center
3220 Campbell Hall
University of California at
 Los Angeles
Los Angeles, CA 90024

AMERICAN INDIAN JOURNAL
Institute for the Development
 of Indian Law
927 15th St., N.W., Suite 200
Washington, DC 20005

AMERICAS (Monthly in Spanish,
 English, and Portuguese)
Organization of American
 States
Pan-American Union
Washington, DC 20006
Juan Villaverde and Flora
 Phelps (eds)

APPALACHIAN OUTLOOK
West Virginia University
 Library, Main Office
Morgantown, WV 26506
Alice L. Dornemann (ed)

THE BILINGUAL JOURNAL
  (Quarterly)
National Assessment and
  Dissemination Center
ESEA Title VII
Lesley College
9 Mellen St.
Cambridge, MA 02138
Antonio Torres-Alcala (ed)

BILNGUAL REVIEW
Bilingual Review Press
York College
Department of Foreign
  Languages
Jamaica, NY 11451
Gary Keller (ed)

BILL OF RIGHTS IN ACTION
  (Quarterly)
(For High School and Adult
  Education)
Constitutional Rights
  Foundation
6310 San Vicente Blvd.
Los Angeles, CA 90048

BLACK AMERICAN LITERATURE
  FORUM
Indiana State University
School of Education
Terre Haute, IN 47809
Joe Weixlmann (ed)

THE BLACK COLLEGIAN
(The National Magazine of
  Black College Students)
Black Collegiate Services,
  Inc.
1240 S. Broad St.
New Orleans, LA 70125
(504) 821-5694
Kalamu ya Salaam (ed)
Note: Subscription
  rate--$7.50

BLACK ENTERPRISE
Earl G. Graves Publishing Co.
295 Madison Ave.
New York, NY 10017
Phil W. Petrie (ed)

BLACK SCHOLAR
Black World Foundation
Box 908
Sausalito, CA 94965

THE BRIDGE: A JOURNAL OF
  CROSS-CULTURAL AFFAIRS
  (Quarterly)
The Center for Research and
  Education
2010 E. 17th Ave.
Denver, CO 80206
(303) 388-6311
Collins Reynolds (ed)

BULLETIN OF THE CANADIAN
  ETHNIC STUDIES ASSOCIATION
Canadian Ethnic Studies
  Association
Department of History
University of Ottawa
147 Wilbrod St.
Ottawa, Ontario K 1G 6N5
Dr. C. J. Jaenen (ed)

CHILDHOOD EDUCATION
Association for Childhood
  Education International
3615 Wisconsin Avenue, N.W.
Washington, DC 20016
Lucy Martin (ed)

CHRYSALIS (Quarterly)
(A Magazine of Women's
  Culture)
Chrysalis
1727 N. Spring St.
Los Angeles, CA 90012
Kirsten Grimstad (ed)

CITIZEN EDUCATION
Research For Better Schools,
  Inc.
444 N. Third St.
Philadelphia, PA 19123

CIVIL RIGHTS DIGEST
Editor, Civil Rights Digest
U.S. Commission on Civil
  Rights
Washington, DC 20425
Suzanne Crowell (ed)

CIVIL RIGHTS UPDATE
U.S. Commission On Civil
  Rights
Washington, DC 20425
Roy Johnson (ed)

COMMENT (ON RESEARCH/ACTION
  ABOUT WOMEN) (3 times per
  year)
National Institute of
  Education and Office of Women
  in Higher Education
One Dupont Circle
Washington, DC 20036
Jo Hartley (ed)

COMMUNICATION QUARTERLY
Institute for Research on
  Teaching
College of Education
Michigan State University
East Lansing, MI 48824
Linda D. F. Shalaway (ed)

CORE MAGAZINE (Congress of
  Racial Equality)
CORE Publications
200 West 135 St.
New York, NY 10030
Denise Mitchell (ed)

DIALOGO (Quarterly)
Center For Latin American
  Studies
University of Florida
Gainesville, FL 32611
Miriam Ocasio (ed)

EAST-WEST CENTER MAGAZINE
Office of Publication and
  Public Affairs
East-West Center
1777 East-West Road
Honolulu, HI 96822
Mark E. Zeug (ed)

LA EDUCACION (Annually in
  Spanish)
Organization of American
  States
Education Department
Washington, DC 20006
Francisco Iglesias (ed)

EDUCATION AND URBAN SOCIETY
Sage Publications Inc.
275 South Beverly Drive
Beverly Hills, CA 90212

EPIC (Biannual Newsletter)
Northeastern State University
Tahlequah, OK 74464
Fount Holland, Wathene Young,
  and Bill Thorne (eds)

EQUAL OPPORTUNITY FORUM
  (Monthly)
Equal Opportunity Forum, Inc.
8240 Beverly Boulevard
Los Angeles, CA 90048
(213) 651-5617
Max Benavidez and Kathleen
  Vozoff (eds)

EQUAL OPPORTUNITY REVIEW
Institute for Urban and
 Minority Education
Teachers College
Columbia University
New York, NY 10027

ETHNICITY (an
 interdisciplinary journal of
 the study of ethnic
 relations)
Academic Press, Inc.
111 Fifth Avenue
New York, NY 10003
Andrew M. Greeley (ed)

THE EXCHANGE (A Quarterly
 Journal of Native
 American-Philanthropic News)
Native American-Philanthropic
 News Service
Phelps-Stokes Fund
1029 Vermont Avenue, N.W.
Washington, DC 20005
Rose Robinson (ed)

FOCUS ON POVERTY RESEARCH
 (Newsletter, three times per
 year)
Institute for Research on
 Poverty
3412 Social Science Bldg.
University of Wisconsin at
 Madison
Madison, WI 53706
Katherine Mochon (ed)

FOMENTO LITERARIO (Spanish and
 English Articles)
El Congreso Nacional de
 Asuntos Colegiales
One Dupont Circle, NW Rm 410
Washington, DC 20036
Pepe Barron (ed)

FORUM (Newsletter)
National Clearinghouse for
 Bilingual Education
1300 Wilson Boulevard, Suite
 B2-11
Rosslyn, VA 22209
Bettie Baca-Fierro (ed)

HISPANA
American Association of
 Teachers of Spanish and
 Portuguese
Department of Modern Languages
Holy Cross College
Worcester, MA 01610
Donald W. Bleznick (ed)

HISPANIC AMERICAN HISTORICAL
 REVIEW
Duke University Press
Box 6697
College Station
Durham, NC 27708
Michael C. Meyer (ed)

HUMAN RESOURCES ABSTRACTS
Sage Publications Inc.
275 South Beverly Drive
Beverly Hills, CA 90212

HUMANIDADES (Quarterly
 Newsletter)
Puerto Rico Endowment For The
 Humanities
P.O. Box S-4307
San Juan, PR 00904
Francisco J. Carreras
 (President)

I.C.E.E. HERITAGE (Newsletter)
Illinois Consultation on
 Ethnicity in Education
Institute on Pluralism and
 Group Identity
55 East Jackson Blvd., Suite
 1880
Chicago, IL 60604
Nancy J. Siatka Rogalla (ed)

ICP NEWSLETTER (Bimonthly
 Newsletter)
Institute for Cultural
 Pluralism
5544 1/2 Hardy Ave.
San Diego, CA 92182
Ricardo Cornejo and Margarita
 Calderon (eds)

IDRA NEWSLETTER (Monthly)
Intercultural Development and
 Research Association
5835 Callaghan Rd., Suite 350
San Antonio, TX 58228
(512) 684-8180
Jose A. Cardenas (ed)

IN THE RUNNING (Newsletter)
SPRINT (A National
 Clearinghouse of Information
 on Sex Equity in Sports)
805 15th St., NW, Suite 822
Washington, DC 20005
(202) 638-1961
Carol Parr (Executive
 Director)

INEQUALITY IN EDUCATION
Center for Law and Education,
 Inc.
Gutman Library
6 Appian Way
Cambridge, MA 02138
Sharon Schumack (ed)

INTEGRATED EDUCATION
 (Bimonthly)
School of Education
Northwestern University
2003 Sheridan Rd.
Evanston, IL 60201
(312) 492-9465
Meyer Weinberg (ed)

INTERNATIONAL AND
 INTERCULTURAL COMMUNICATION
 ANNUAL
Speech Communication
 Association
Statler Hilton Hotel
New York, NY 10001

INTERNATIONAL JOURNAL OF
 INTERCULTURAL RELATIONS
Pergamon Press, Inc.
Fairview Park
Elmsford, NY 10523
Dan Landis (ed)

INTERNATIONAL MIGRATION REVIEW
 (Quarterly)
Center for Migration Studies
209 Flagg Place
Staten Island, NY 10304

INTERRACIAL BOOKS FOR CHILDREN
 BULLETIN
Council on Interracial Books
 for Children
1841 Broadway
New York, NY 10023
Bradford Chambers (ed)

INTERRACIAL DIGEST
Council on Interracial Books
 for Children
1841 Broadway
New York, NY 10023
Ruth Charnes (ed)

IRCD BULLETIN
Institute for Urban and
 Minority Education
Teachers College
Columbia University
Box 40, 525 West 120th St.
New York, NY 10027
Edmund W. Gordon (ed)

JEWISH EDUCATION
National Council for Jewish
 Education
114 Fifth Ave.
New York, NY 10011
Alvin Schiff (ed)

JOURNAL OF AFRO-AMERICAN
 ISSUES
Educational and Community
 Counselors Associates
1629 K St., NW, Suite 520
Washington, DC 20006

JOURNAL OF AMERICAN INDIAN
 EDUCATION
Arizona State University
College of Education
Bureau of Educational Research
 and Services
Tempe, AZ 85281
George A. Gill (ed)

JOURNAL OF BLACK STUDIES
Sage Publications, Inc.
275 S. Beverly Dr.
Beverly Hills, CA 90212
Molefi Kete (ed)

JOURNAL OF ETHNIC STUDIES
Western Washington University
College of Ethnic Studies
Bellingham, WA 98225
Jeffrey D. Wilner and Jesse
 Hiraoka (eds)

JOURNAL OF INTERGROUP
 RELATIONS
National Association of Human
 Rights Workers
526 West 39th St.
Kansas City, MO 64111
Griffin Crump (ed)

THE JOURNAL OF NEGRO EDUCATION
Howard University Press
Howard University
Washington, DC 20059
Charles A. Martin (ed)

JOURNAL OF NEGRO HISTORY
Association for the Study of
 Afro-American Life and
 History
1407 14th St., NW
Washington, DC 20005
Alton Hornsby (ed)

JOURNAL OF NON-WHITE CONCERNS
 IN PERSONNEL AND GUIDANCE
American Personnel and
 Guidance Association
1607 New Hampshire Ave., NW
Washington, DC 20009
Ed Maggie (ed)

JOURNAL OF TEACHER EDUCATION
American Association of
 Colleges for Teacher
 Education
One Dupont Circle, Suite 610
Washington, DC 20036
(202) 293-2450
Martin Haberman (ed)

LATCA (A Magazine of Latino
  Awareness in the Midwest)
Indiana University
LaCasa/Latino Center
Bloomington, IN 47401
(812) 337-0174
Jack Ramos Needham (ed)

LAW AND CONTEMPORARY PROBLEMS
Duke University School of Law
Duke University Press
Durham, NC 27706
Melvin G. Shimm

LEGAL MEMORANDUM
National Association of
  Secondary School Principals
1904 Association Dr.
Reston, VA 22091
Thomas F. Koerner (ed)

THE LINGUISTIC REPORTER
  (Newsletter)
Center for Applied Linguistics
1611 N. Kent St.
Arlington, VA 22209
(703) 528-4312
JoAnn Crandall (ed)

METAS
Aspira of America
205 Lexington Ave.
New York, NY 10016
Kal Wagenheim (ed)

MEXICAN NEWSLETTER (Monthly)
Mexican Newletter
Palma No. 40-5o. piso
Mexico 1, D.F., Mexico

MIGRATION TODAY (Bimonthly
  Newsletter)
Center for Migration Studies
209 Flagg Place
Staten Island
New York, NY 10304

MINORITY NEWS DIGEST
Minority News Digest, Inc.
No. 2 East 37th St.
New York, NY 10016
(212) 683-6363
Clemencio A. McKoy (ed)

MONITOR
Institute for the Study of
  Educational Policy
2935 Upton St., NW
Washington, DC 20008
Earnestine Stripling (ed)

MOSAIC
Institute of Intercultural
  Relations and Ethnic Studies
Rutgers University, GSE
10 Seminary Place
New Brunswick, NJ 08903
Eliane C. Condon and Madelyn
  Milchman (ed)

MULTICULTURALISM (Quarterly)
University of Toronto Faculty
  of Education and the
  Multicultural Development
  Branch of the Ministry of
  Culture and Recreation of
  Ontario
371 Bloor St., West
Toronto, Ontario, Canada M4W
  2K8
Keith A. McLeod (ed)

NEA REPORTER
National Education Association
1201 16th St., NW
Washington, DC 20036
Marshall O. Donley, Jr.(ed)

NEGRO EDUCATIONAL REVIEW
Box 2895
West Bay Annex
Jacksonville, FL 32216
R. Grann Lloyd (ed)

NETWORK (Quarterly)
National Urban Coalition
1201 Connecticut Ave., NW
Washington, DC 20036
(202) 331-2413
Stephanie Drea (ed)

NEW DIRECTIONS (Quarterly)
Howard University
Department of University
 Relations and Publications
Washington, DC 20059
Abdulkadir N. Said (ed)

NEWSLETTER
Asian American Bilingual
 Center
2168 Shattuck Ave., 3/F
Berkeley, CA 94704
Note: ESEA Publication, Title
VII National Network of
Centers for Bilingual
Education

NEWSNOTES
The Feminist Press
Box 334
Old Westbury, NY 11568
Phyllis Arlow (ed)
Note: Irregular Publication

PEER PERSPECTIVE
Project on Equal Education
 Rights
1029 Vermont Ave., NW, Suite
 800
Washington, DC 20005
(202) 332-7337
Robin Gordon (ed)

RACE AND CLASS
Institute of Race Relations
247 Pentonville Rd.
London 1, England
A. Sivanandan (ed)

REPORT CARD ON INTEGRATION
 (Monthly Newsletter)
The Center for the Advancement
 of Integrated Education
7 East 96th St.
New York, NY 10028

REPORT ON EDUCATION RESEARCH
Capitol Publications, Inc.
Suite G-12, 2430 Pennsylvania
 Ave., NW
Washington, DC 20037
(202) 452-1600
Emily C. Harris (ed)

REPORT ON THE EDUCATION OF THE
 DISADVANTAGED
Capitol Publications, Inc.
Education News Services
 Division
Suite G-12, 2430 Pennsylvania
 Ave., NW
Washington, DC 20037
Helen Hoart (ed)

RESEARCH REVIEW OF EQUAL
 EDUCATION (Quarterly)
Center for Equal Education
School of Education
University of Massachusetts
Amherst, MA 01003
(413) 545-0327
Meyer Weinberg (ed)

SCHOOLS and CIVIL RIGHTS NEWS
 (Biweekly Newsletter)
Capitol Publications, Inc.
Suite G-12, 2430 Pennsylvania
 Ave., NW
Washington, DC 20037
Emily C. Harris (ed)

SEX ROLES: A JOURNAL OF
  RESEARCH
Plenum Press
227 W. 17th St.
New York, NY 10011
Phyllis A. Katz (ed)

SIETAR COMMUNIQUE (Quarterly
  Newsletter)
Society for Intercultural
  Education, Training, and
  Research
Georgetown University
Washington, DC 20057
Diane L. Zeller (ed)

SOCIAL EDUCATION
National Council for the
  Social Studies
1515 Wilson Blvd.
Arlington, VA 22209
Daniel Roselle (ed)

SOCIAL POLICY
Social Policy Corp.
Suite 500, 184 Fifth Ave.
New York, NY 10010
Frank Riessman (ed)

SPECTRUM
Immigration History Research
  Center
University of Minnesota
826 Berry St.
St. Paul, MN 55114
Michael G. Karni (ed)

TEACHING EXCEPTIONAL CHILDREN
Council for Exceptional
  Children
1920 Association Dr.
Reston, VA 22091
June B. Jordan (ed)

T.E.S.O.L. QUARTERLY
Teachers of English to
  Speakers of Other Languages
c/o James E. Alatis
School of Languages and
  Linguistics
Georgetown University
Washington, DC 20057

UN NUEVO DIA
The Chicano Education Project
5410 W. Mississippi
Lakewood, CO 80226
(303) 922-6371
Nancy De La Rosa and Lydia
  Urioste (eds)

URBAN AFFAIRS QUARTERLY
Sage Publications, Inc.
275 S. Beverly Dr.
Beverly Hills, CA 90212
Louis Masotti (ed)

URBAN EDUCATION
Sage Publications, Inc.
275 S. Beverly Dr.
Beverly Hills, cA 90212
Warren Button (ed)

URBAN LIFE (A JOURNAL OF
  ETHNOGRAPHIC RESEARCH)
Sage Publications, Inc.
275 S. Beverly Dr.
Beverly Hills, CA 90212
Peter Manning (ed)

URBAN REVIEW
APS Publications
150 Fifth Ave.
New York, NY 10011
David E. Kapel and William
  T. Pink (eds)

WOMEN TODAY
Today Publications and News
 Service, Inc.
621 National Press Bldg.
Washington, DC 20045
Myra E. Barrer (ed)

WOMEN'S WORK
Women's Work, Inc.
1302 18th St., NW, Suite 203
Washington, DC 20036

Part 2: Funding Resources

Annual Register of Grant Support
    Marquis Who's Who, Inc., 200 East Ohio St., Chicago, IL 60611 (312) 787-2008.

    Available in libraries and college research offices. Complete descriptions of more than 2300 current grant programs.

The Art of Writing Successful R and D Proposals by Donald
    C. Orlich and Patricia Rend Orlich. $9.40.
    Redgrave Publishing Company, 430 Manville, NJ 10570 (914) 769-3629

    A tested guide to getting grants. Includes what to consider in writing proposals, how to write them, and where to present them.

The Bread Game: The Realities of Foundation Fundraising. $2.00.
    Glide Publications, 330 Ellis, San Francisco, CA 94102 (415) 775-0918.

    Recommends steps to take in approaching foundations and practices of grants administration.

Catalog of Federal Domestic Assistance.
    Superintendent of Documents, Government Printing Office, Washington, DC 20402 (202) 783-3238.

    Available in public libraries and college research offices. A valuable sourcebook for anyone seeking federal support funds. Contains a listing and description of all federal programs and activities that provide grants or other assistance or benefits to the American public. Information includes purpose, who may apply, where to apply or get additional information, past awards. Published yearly.

Commerce Business Daily.
   Superintendent of Documents, Government Printing Office, Washington, DC 20402 (202) 783-3238.

   Available in public libraries. Daily publication of federal government procurement information, including Requests for Proposals and announcements of upcoming research, development and training awards. Does not cover grants for research or educational programs, only contracts.

Developing Skills in Proposal Writing by Mary Hall. 1979.
   Continuing Education Publications, P.O. Box 1491, Portland, OR 97207 (503) 229-4843.

   Instructions for assessing the strengths, abilities, and credibility of the potential grantee. Guidance and definitions of the materials that should be included in the statement of the goals, objectives, and hypothesis.

Directory of Research Grants.
   ORYX Press, 3930 East Camelback Rd., Phoenix, AZ 85108 (602) 956-6233.

   Available in library. Published annually. Compilation of grants sources.

Federal Education Grants Directory.
   Capitol Publications, Inc., 2430 Pennsylvania Ave., NW, Washington, DC 20037 (202) 452-1600.

   Programs for the Catalog of Federal Domestic Assistance of significant interest to education administrators. Information on who to contact in DHEW and other federal agencies for funding details. Published annually.

Federal Register.
   Superintendent of Documents, Government Printing Office, Washington, DC 20402 (202) 783-3238.

   Available in libraries and university research offices. Daily publication of notices of legal rules and regulations, as well as application deadlines for new grants programs of all federal agencies. The monthly index may be ordered separately at $8.00 per year.

Federal Grants: A Basic Handbook.
Association of American Colleges, Federal Resources Advisory Services, 1818 R St., NW, Washington, DC 20009 (202) 387-3760.

Overview of grantsmanship process. Stresses information gathering, contacts with Washington and proposal writing.

Federal Grants and Contracts Weekly.
Capitol Publications, Inc., 2430 Pennsylvania Ave., NW, Washington, DC 20037 (202) 452-1600.

Selected opportunities for the education community.

Foundation Directory. $40.00.
Columbia University Press, 136 S. Broadway, Irvington-on-Hudson, NY 10533 (914) 591-9370.

Available in libraries. Lists nonprofit, nongovernmental foundations that make grants of at least $25,000 a year or have assets of a least $500,000. Includes names, addresses, purposes, and activities of donor, current officers, trustees, and directors of each foundation.

Foundation Grants Index.
Columbia University Press, 136 S. Broadway, Irvington-on-Hudson, NY 10533 (914) 591-9370.

Available in libraries. Lists current grants of at least $5,000.

Foundation News. $20.00 annually (six issues).
Council on Foundations, 1828 L St., NW, Washington, DC 20036 (202) 466-6512.

Articles and reports on grant-making; includes "Foundation Grants Index."

Fund Raising by Parent/Citizen Groups, 1977. $1.75.
National Committee for Citizens in Education, Wilde Lake Village Green, Suite 410, Columbia, MD 21044.

Grants: How to Find Out About Them and What to Do Next, 1978. $19.95.
Learning Concepts, 2501 N. Lamar, Austin, TX 78705 (512) 747-6911.

What grants are, who gives them, who gets them; the first step; writing grant proposals. List of sources.

Grantsmanship: Money and How to Get It, 1978. $7.50.
Marquis Who's Who, Inc., 200 East Ohio St., Chicago, IL 60611 (312) 787-2008.

Tells how to define project goals, locate potential donors, research specific programs, write letters of inquiry, prepare formal proposals, report results.

The Grass Roots Fund Raising Book: How to Raise Money in Your Community. $5.25.
Swallow Press, P.O. Box 988, Hicksville, NY 11802.

Ideas about local fund-raising, an alternative to federal or foundation funds.

Guide to Office of Education Programs. Free.
U.S. Office of Education, Washington, DC 20202 (202) 245-8707.

Summary of all USOE programs of financial support, including grants for research and development; type and purpose of assistance; authorizing legislation; appropriation by Congress; who may apply, and where to apply. Each federal agency, and often the different program units within each agency, will also usually publish announcements and guidelines. These publications describe specific subjects for which proposals will be considered, and give instructions for preparing and submitting proposals to the issuing agency.

How to Get Government Grants, by Philip Des Marais. $13.50.
Capitol Publications, 2430 Pennsylvania Ave., NW, Washington, DC 20037 (202) 452-1600.

How eligible institutions must be organized for government funding. Description of special system for grant management when funding has been received.

<u>How to Prepare a Research Proposal</u> by David R. Krathwohl. Syracuse University Bookstore, 303 University Place, Syracuse, NY 13210 (315) 423-2426.

Information for educators and behavioral scientists seeking support for basic research.

Part 3: Special Articles and Issues

"America's Children: Bilingual/Multicultural Education--Hope for the Culturally Alienated," NATIONAL EDUCATION ASSOCIATION REPORTER, Vol. 15, No. 4, April 1976. Special Issue.

"Assessing Race Relations in the Classroom," ANTHROPOLOGY AND EDUCATION QUARTERLY, Vol. VIII, No. 2, May 1977, pp. 142-161. Feature Section.

"Bilingual Education: Whose Heritage Is Being Prized?" LEARNING, October 1976. Special Issue.

"The Courts, Social Science and School Desegregation," LAW AND CONTEMPORARY PROBLEMS, Vol. 39, No. 1, Winter 1975, and No. 2, Spring 1975. Special Issues.

"Cultural Pluralism: Educational Concepts, Conflicts, & Consequences," EDUCATIONAL RESEARCH QUARTERLY, Vol. 2, No. 24, Winter 1978. Special Issue.

"Desegregation in the 1970s: A Candid Discussion," THE JOURNAL OF NEGRO EDUCATION, Vol. 4, No. 1. Winter 1978.

"Early Childhood: The Best time To Become Bilingual and Biliterate," CHILDHOOD EDUCATION, Vol. 54, No. 3, January 1978. Special Issue.

"Education and Ethnicity," CANADIAN ETHNIC STUDIES, Vol. III, No. 1, 1978. Special Issue.

"Education in the Soviet Union," COMMUNICATION QUARTERLY, Vol. 2, No. 2, Winter 1979. Special Issue.

"Ethnicity in a Contemporary Society: Toward the Development of a Typology," by James A Banks and Geneva Gay, ETHNICITY, Vol. 5, 1978. (pp. 238-251).

"ERIC Reference on Urban and Minority Education," EQUAL OPPORTUNITY REVIEW, May 1979. Special Issue.

"Ethnic and Multiethnic Studies in the Schools," THRESHOLDS IN EDUCATION, Vol. III, No. 4, November 1977. Special Issue.

"Ethnic Studies as a Process of Curriculum Reform," SOCIAL EDUCATION, Vol. 40, No. 2, February 1976. Special Issue.

"Feminism: Role Playing or Realism," THE DELTA KAPPA GAMMA BULLETIN, Vol. XLIII-4, Summer 1977. Special Issue.

"The Future Will Demand Culturally Literate Citizens" by Carlos Cortes, THRUST FOR EDUCATIONAL LEADERSHIP, Vol. 7, No. 3, January 1978.

"Glimpses of Education in Poland and Romania" by Gertrude Mitchell, AMERICAN EDUCATION, Vol. 13, No. 3, April 1977. Special Article.

"Immigrants and Religion: The Persistence of Ethnic Diversity," SPECTRUM, (Immigration Research Center, Univ of Mich.), Vol. 1, No. 3. Special Issue.

"The Implications of Regents of California vs. Bakke for University Admission and Hiring," EQUAL OPPORTUNITY REVIEW (ERIC Clearinghouse on Urban Education), February 1979. Special Issue.

"Improving Teacher Awareness of Ethnic Life Styles" by Fonda L. Chaffee, EDUCATIONAL LEADERSHIP, Vol. 33, No. 2, November 1975. Special Article.

"Interracial Contact and Student Prejudice" by Charles S. Bullock, III, YOUTH & SOCIETY, Vol. 7, No. 3, March 1976.

"Isolation of Negro Students in Integrated Public Schools" by Morrill M. Hall & Harold W. Gentry, JOURNAL OF NEGRO EDUCATION, Howard University.

"Is School Desegregation Still a Good Idea? THE UNIVERSITY OF CHICAGO SCHOOL REVIEW, Vol. 84, No. 4, May 1976. Special Issue. 1051

"Just Schools," SOUTHERN EXPOSURE, Vol. VII, No. 2, Summer 1979. Special Issue.

"Language and Culture," MOSAIC, Vol. 4, No. 1, (Fall) and No. 2 (Winter), 1979. Special Issues.

"Meeting the Challenge of Multicultural Pluralism," MOMENTUM (Journal of the National Catholic Educational Association), Vol. VI, No. 3, October 1975. Special Issue.

"The Molding of the Non-Sexist Teacher," JOURNAL OF TEACHER EDUCATION, Vol. XXVI, No. 4, Winter 1975. Special Issue.

"Multicultural Education," ANTHROPOLOGY AND EDUCATION QUARTERLY, Vol. 7, 1976.

"Multicultural Education," JOURNAL OF RESEARCH AND DEVELOPMENT IN EDUCATION Vol. 11, No. 1, Fall 1977. Special Isssue.

"Multicultural Education: Teaching About Minority Women," Special Current Issues Publication No. 8, ERIC Clearinghouse on Teacher Education.

"Multicultural Education and the Disciplines," JOURNAL OF TEACHER EDUCATION, Vol. 28, No. 3, May-June 1977. Special Issue.

"Multicultural Education in the International Year of the Child: Problems and Possibilities," THE JOURNAL OF NEGRO EDUCATION, Vol. 48, No. 3, Summer 1979. Special Issue.

"The Multicultural Learner," THE LEARNER IN THE PROCESS, Vol. 1, No. 11, Fall 1978. Special Issue.

"Multiculturalism in Contemporary Education," VIEWPOINTS IN TEACHING AND LEARNING, Vol. 56, No. 1, Winter 1980. Special Issue.

"Multiethnic Education in Five Lands," SOCIAL EDUCATION, Vol. 42, No. 3, March 1978. Special Issue.

"Multi-Ethnic Literature," ILLINOIS SCHOOLS JOURNAL, Vol. 56, Fall 1975. Special Issue.

"The 'New' Multicultural Social Studies Curriculum" by Eleanor Blumenberg, SOCIAL STUDIES REVIEW, Vol. 18, No. 1, Fall 1978.

"No One Model American," THE UNIVERSITY OF TOLEDO COLLEGE OF EDUCATION: EDUCATIONAL COMMENT, 1979. Special Issue.

"On Multicultural Education" by Carlos E. Cortes, THRUST FOR EDUCATIONAL LEADERSHIP, Vol. 7, No. 3, 1978.

"Overcoming Sex-Role Stereotypes," CHILDHOOD EDUCATION, Vol. 52, No. 4, February 1976. Special Issue. "Para un Neuvo Dia en la Educacíon (Toward a New Era in Education): The Chicano Education Project, CARNEGIE QUARTERLY, Vol. XXVI, No. 4, Winter 1979. Special Issue.

"Policy Implications of Cross-National Education Surveys" by Torsten Husen, NEW YORK UNIVERSITY EDUCATION QUARTERLY, Vol. VII, No. 3, Spring 1976. Special Issue.

"Prospectus on Black Communications" by Clifford Carter, THE SCHOOL PSYCHOLOGY DIGEST, Vol. 6, No. 3, Winter 1977. Special Article.

"A Rationale for Including Multicultural Education and its Implementation in the Daily Lesson Plan" by Charles Payne, JOURNAL OF RESEARCH AND DEVELOPMENT IN EDUCATION, Vol. II, No. 1, 1977.

"School Desegregation in Metropolitan Areas: Choices and Prospects," THE URBAN REVIEW, Vol. 10, No. 2, Summer 1978. Special Issue.

"School Desegregation: Outcomes for Children (Findings in a Search of a Theory)" by Nancy H. St. John, IRCD BULLETIN, Vol. XIII, No. 2, Spring 1978. Special Issue.

"Selected Aspects of Multicultural Education," EDUCATIONAL PERSPECTIVES, Vol. 16, No. 4, December 1977. Special Issue.

"Sexism and Racism: Feminist Perspectives," CIVIL RIGHTS DIGEST, Vol. 6, No. 3, Spring 1974. Special Issue.

"Symposium Issue on School Desegregation," SOCIAL POLICY, January-February 1976, Vol. 6, No. 4. Special Issue.

"A Statistical Study of the English Syntax of Bilingual Mexican American and Monolingual Anglo American Students" by Raymond J. Rodrigues, THE BILINGUAL REVIEW (LA REVISTA BILINGUE), Vol. III, No. 3, September-December 1976.

"Women and Minorities in School Administration," by David Coursen, SCHOOL LEADERSHIP DIGEST. Special Article. (ED 102640).

"Women In Search of Equality," FOCUS, No. 6, 1979. Special Issue.

Section III

ORGANIZATION RESOURCES

THE AFRICAN-AMERICAN INSTITUTE
833 United Nations Plaza
New York, NY 10017
(212) 949-5666
Contact: Donald Easum,
 President

ALASKAN NATIVE LANGUAGE
 MATERIAL DEVELOPMENT CENTER
University of Alaska
2223 Spenard Rd.
Anchorage, AK 99503
(907) 276-0547
Contact: Tupou Pulu

AMANECER (Multicultural Action
 Network for Early Childhood
 Educational Resources)
I.D.R.A.
5835 Callaghan Rd., Suite 350
San Antonio, TX 78228 Contact:
 Jose A. Cardenas, Executive
 Director

AMERICAN ASSOCIATION OF
 UNIVERSITY WOMEN
2401 Virginia Ave., NW,
Washington, DC 20037

THE AMERICAN HUNGARIAN
 EDUCATOR'S ASSOCIATION
707 Snider Lane
Silver Spring, MD 20904
(301) 426-6323
Contact: Eniko M. Base

AMERICAN INDIAN STUDIES CENTER
(Native North American
 Languages)
University of California
Campbell Hall, Rm. 3220
405 Hilgard Ave.
Los Angeles, CA 90024
(213) 825-7315
Contact: Karin Abbey

ANTI-DEFAMATION LEAGUE OF
 B'NAI B'RITH
315 Lexington Ave.
New York, NY 10016

ARIZONA TITLE VII BILINGUAL
 MATERIALS DEVELOPMENT CENTER
College of Education
Box 601
University of Arizona
Tucson, AZ 85721
(602) 626-1618

ARMENIAN LANGUAGE LAB AND
 RESOURCE CENTER
Diocese of the Armenian Church
 of America
630 Second Ave.
New York, NY 10016
(212) 696-0710
Contact: Sylva Der Stepanian

ASIAN AMERICAN BILINGUAL
 CENTER
2168 Shattuck Avenue
Berkeley, CA 94704

ASIAN BILINGUAL CURRICULUM
  DEVELOPMENT CENTER (CHINESE)
Seton Hall University
440 South Orange Ave.
South Orange, NJ 07070
(201) 762-9000 or 762-4973
Contact: John Young

ASSOCIATION FOR CHILDHOOD
  EDUCATION INTERNATIONAL
3615 Wisconsin Ave., N.W.
Washington, DC 20016

ASSOCIATION FOR SUPERVISION &
  CURRICULUM DEVELOPMENT
225 N. Washington Street
Alexandria, VA 2314

ASSOCIATION OF AMERICAN INDIAN
  AFFAIRS, INC.
432 Park Ave., South
New York, NY 10016

BAY AREA BILINGUAL EDUCATION
  LEAGUE (BABEL) (Title
  VII--Material in East Asian
  Languages)
2168 Shattuck Ave.
Berkeley, CA 94704
(415) 549-1820
Contact: George Yoshida and
  Linda Wing

BILINGUAL BICULTURAL EDUCATION
  OFFICE
(Title VII--Materials in East
  Asian Languages)
Oakland Unified School
  District
821 East 14th
Oakland, CA 94606
(415) 836-2622, exts. 753,
  786, 806
Contact: Josephine Lee

BILINGUAL BICULTURAL EDUCATION
  (Title VII Tagalog Center)
Oakland Unified School
  District
831 East 14th
Oakland, CA 94606
(415) 836-2622 exts. 753, 786,
  806, 852
Contact: Enriqueta Tiangsing

BILINGUAL EDUCATION FOR
  COMMUNITY SCHOOL DISTRICT #21
  (Title VII Hebrew Center)
345 Van Sickle St.
Brooklyn, NY 11223
(212) 266-1733
Contact: Ms. Gina Sullivan,
  Superintendent

BILINGUAL OFFICE (Title VII,
  Pennsylvania Dutch)
Lancaster-Lebanon Intermediate
  Unit No. 13
1110 Enterprise Road
East Petersburg, PA 17520
(717) 354-4601
Contact: Carolyn Ebel

BILINGUAL RESOURCE CENTER
  (Title VII)
Box 4-3410
University of Southern
  Louisiana
Lafayette, LA 70504
(318) 264-6000
Contact: Ruth Bradey (French)
  & Ralph Foriestieri
  (Italian/Hungarian)

BOSTON PUBLIC SCHOOLS
Department of Bilingual
  Education
26 Court St., 8th Floor
Boston, MA 02108
(617) 726-6296
Contact: Rafael De Gruttola

BOSTON PUBLIC SCHOOLS (Greek)
Title VII Office
26 Court St., 8th Floor
Boston, MA 02108
(617) 726-6323
Contact: Carol Snyder

CENTER FOR APPLIED
 LINGUISTICS
1611 North Kent St.
Arlington, VA 22209
(703) 528-4312
Contact: Rudolph C. Troike,
 Director

THE CENTER FOR THE ADVANCEMENT
 OF INTEGRATED EDUCATION
7 East 96th St.
New York, NY 10028

CENTER FOR MIGRATION STUDIES
209 Flagg Place
Staten Island, NY 10304
Publishers of INTERNATIONAL
 MIGRATION REVIEW (Quarterly)
 and MIGRATION TODAY
 (Bimonthly)

CENTER FOR TEACHING
 INTERNATIONAL RELATIONS
Graduate School of
 International Studies
University of Denver
Denver, CO 80210

CENTER FOR THE STUDY OF
 EVALUATION
145 Moore Hall
University of California
Los Angeles, CA 90024

CENTER FOR VIETNAMESE STUDIES
Pulliam Hall
Southern Illinois University
Carbondale, IL 62901
(618) 536-3385
Contact: Dinh-Hoa Nguyen

CHICANO STUDIES CENTER
University of California at
 Los Angeles
Los Angeles, CA 90024
Publishers of AZTLAN and
 INTERNATIONAL JOURNAL OF
CHICANO STUDIES MONOGRAPHS

THE COALITION RESOURCE CENTER
 (Native North American
 Languages)
Coalition of Indian Controlled
 School Boards
511 16th St.
Denver, CO 80202
(303) 573-5715

COMMISSION FOR RACIAL EQUALITY
Elliot House
10-12 Allington Street
London SW1E 5EH

COMMUNITY RELATIONS COMMISSION
15-16 Bedford Street
London WC2E 9HX

COUNCIL FOR EXCEPTIONAL
 CHILDREN
1920 Association Drive
Reston, VA 22091

COUNCIL ON ANTHROPOLOGY AND
 EDUCATION
American Anthropological
 Association
1703 New Hampshire Ave., NW
Washington, DC 20009
(202) 232-8800

COUNCIL ON INTERRACIAL BOOKS
  FOR CHILDREN
1841 Broadway
New York, NY 10023

THE DANISH BROTHERHOOD IN
  AMERICA
Fraternal Affairs Department
3717 Harney St.
Omaha, NE 68131
(402) 341-5049

DATA USE AND ACCESS
  LABORATORIES, INC.
National Ethnic Statistical
  Data Guidance Service
1601 North Kent St.
Arlington, VA 22209
(703) 525-1480

DEARBORN PUBLIC SCHOOLS
Bilingual Office, Title VII
4824 Lois Ave.
Dearborn, MI 48126
(313) 582-7160
Contact: Frances Haddad

DENOYER-GEPPERT CO.
5235 Ravenswood Ave.
Chicago, IL 60640

DESIGN ENTERPRISES OF SAN
  FRANCISCO
PO Box 27677
San Francisco, CA 94127

DISSEMINATION & ASSESSMENT
  CENTER (Title VII, Alaskan
  and Indian Languages)
7703 North Lamar Boulevard
Austin, TX 78752
(512) 458-9131
Contact: Carlos Perez

THE DISSEMINATION CENTER FOR
  THE PRODUCTS OF THE WOMEN'S
  EDCATIONAL EQUITY ACT PROGRAM
  (U.S. Department of HEW,
  Office of Education)
c/o Education Development
  Center
55 Chapel St.
Newton, MA 02160
(617) 969-7100 Or toll free
  (800) 225-3088

DOUGLAS SCHOOL DISTRICT ST-1
  (Title VII, Thai)
Box Elder, SD 57706
(605) 923-1431
Contact: Tongda Rugsaken

EAST-WEST CENTER
East-West Culture Learning
  Institute
Honolulu, Hawaii 96848

EDUCATIONAL PRODUCTS
  INFORMATION EXCHANGE
  INSTITUTE (EPIE)
475 Riverside Drive
New York, NY 10027
(212) 866-3600, 870-2330
Contact: P. Kenneth Komoski,
  Executive Director

EL MUSEO DEL BARRIO
1945 Third Ave.
New York, NY 10029

ERIC (EDUCATIONAL RESOURCES
  INFORMATION CENTER)
U.S. Department of Health,
  Education & Welfare,
National Institute of
  Education
Washington, DC 20208

ERIC CLEARINGHOUSE ON ADULT,
   CAREER, & VOCATIONAL
   EDUCATION
Ohio State University
National Center for Research
   in Vocational Education
1960 Kenny Rd.
Columbus, OH 43210
(614) 486-3655

ERIC CLEARINGHOUSE ON
   COUNSELING & PERSONNEL
   SERVICES
University of Michigan
School of Education Bldg.,
   Rm. 2108
Ann Arbor, MI 48109
(313) 764-9492

ERIC CLEARINGHOUSE ON
   EDUCATIONAL MANAGEMENT
University of Oregon
Eugene, OR 97403
(503) 686-5043

ERIC CLEARINGHOUSE ON
   ELEMENTARY & EARLY CHILDHOOD
   EDUCATION
University of Illinois
College of Education
Urbana, IL 61801
(217) 333-1386

ERIC CLEARINGHOUSE ON
   HANDICAPPED & GIFTED CHILDREN
Council for Exceptional
   Children
1920 Association Dr.
Reston, VA 22091
(703) 620-3660

ERIC CLEARINGHOUSE ON HIGHER
   EDUCATION
George Washington University
One Dupont Circle, Suite 630
Washington, DC 20036
(202) 296-2597

ERIC CLEARINGHOUSE ON
   INFORMATION RESOURCES
Syracuse University
School of Education
130 Huntington Hall
Syracuse, NY 13210
(315) 423-3640

ERIC CLEARINGHOUSE FOR JUNIOR
   COLLEGES
University of California
Powell Library, Rm. 96
405 Hilgard Ave.
Los Angeles, CA 90024
(213) 825-3931

ERIC CLEARINGHOUSE ON
   LANGUAGES & LINGUISTICS
Center for Applied Linguistics
1611 North Kent St.
Arlington, VA 22209
(703) 528-4312

ERIC CLEARINGHOUSE ON READING
   & COMMUNICATION SKILLS
National Council of Teachers
   of English
1111 Kenyon Rd.
Urbana, IL 61801
(217) 328-3870

ERIC CLEARINGHOUSE ON RURAL
   EDUCATION & SMALL SCHOOLS
New Mexico State University
Box 3 AP
Las Cruces, NM 88003
(505) 646-2623

ERIC CLEARINGHOUSE FOR
   SCIENCE, MATHEMATICS, &
   ENVIRONMENTAL EDUCATION
Ohio State University
1200 Chambers Rd., Third Floor
Columbus, OH 43212
(614) 422-6717

ERIC CLEARINGHOUSE FOR SOCIAL
 STUDIES/SOCIAL SCIENCE
 EDUCATION
855 Broadway
Boulder, CO 80302
(303) 492-8434

ERIC CLEARINGHOUSE ON TEACHER
 EDUCATION
American Association of
 Colleges for Teacher
 Education
One Dupont Circle, Suite 616
Washington, DC 20036
(202) 293-2450

ERIC CLEARINGHOUSE ON TESTS,
 MEASUREMENT, & EVALUATION
Educational Testing Service
Rosedale Rd.
Princeton, NJ 08541
(609) 921-9000, ext. 2176

ERIC CLEARINGHOUSE ON URBAN
 EDUCATION
Teachers College, Columbia
 University
Box 40
525 W. 120th St.
New York, NY 10027
(212) 678-3437

ETHNIC HERITAGE STUDIES
 CLEARINGHOUSE
Social Science Education
 Consortium
855 Broadway
Boulder, CO 80302
(303) 492-8154

EDACBE (EVALUATION,
 DISSEMINATION, AND ASSESSMENT
 CENTER FOR BILINGUAL
 EDUCATION, TITLE VII)
7703 North Lamar Boulevard
Austin, TX 78752
(512) 458-9131

FAR WEST LABORATORY FOR
 EDUCATIONAL RESEARCH AND
 DEVELOPMENT
1855 Folsom St.
San Francisco, CA 94103
(415) 565-3000
Contact: John Hemphill,
 Director

FEDERAL COMMUNICATIONS
 COMMISSION
1919 M St., NW
Washington, DC 20554
(202) 632-7260--general info.
(202) 632-0002--for recorded
 listing of releases and texts

THE FEMINIST PRESS
PO Box 334
Old Westbury, NY 11568

FORT HAMILTON HIGH SCHOOL
8301 Shore Road
Brooklyn, NY 11209
(212) 748-1018
Contact: Gertrude Burns

THE FOUNDATION CENTER
1001 Connecticut Ave., NW
Washington, DC 20036
(202) 331-1400

or

888 7th Ave.
New York, NY 10019
(212) 975-1120

FOUNDATION FOR CHANGE, INC.
1841 Broadway
New York, NY 10019

GLIDE PUBLICATIONS/THIRD WORLD
 PUBLICATIONS
330 Ellis Street
San Francisco, CA 94102

HEARTLAND EDUCATION AGENCY
 (Title VII, Laotian)
1932 SW Third St.
Ankeny, IA 50021
(515) 964-2550
Contact: Richard Murphy

IMMIGRATION HISTORY RESEARCH
 CENTER
University of Minnesota
826 Berry St.
St. Paul, MN 55114
(612) 373-5581
Contact: Rudolph J. Vecoli,
 Director

IMPACT PUBLISHERS
PO 1094
San Luis Obispo, CA 93406

THE INDIAN EDUCATION PROGRAM
 (Native North American
 Languages)
Center for Applied Linguistics
1611 North Kent St.
Arlington, VA 22209
(703) 528-4312
Contact: William Leap

INDIAN EDUCATION RESOURCE
 CENTER (Native North American
 Languages)
Indian Education Resource
 Center
Bureau of Indians Affairs
P.O. Box 1788
Albuquerque, NM 87103

INSTITUTE FOR AMERICAN INDIAN
 ARTS
Research and Cultural Studies
Development Section
Cerillos Road
Santa Fe, NM 87501
(505) 988-6486
Contact: Dave Warren

INSTITUTE FOR THE STUDY OF
 EDUCATIONAL POLICY
Howard University, Dumbarton
 Campus
2935 Upton St., NW
Washington, DC 20008
(202) 686-6686
Contact: Paul Brock

INSTITUTE ON PLURALISM AND
 GROUP IDENTITY
The American Jewish Committee
165 East 56th St.
New York, NY 10022

INTERCULTURAL DEVELOPMENT
 RESEARCH ASSOCIATES
5835 Callaghan Road, Suite 350
San Antonio, TX 78228

INTERCULTURAL NETWORK, INC.
906 North Spring Ave.
LaGrange Park, IL 60525
(312) 579-0646
Contact: Margaret D. Pusch,
 Executive Director

INTERNATIONAL CENTER FOR
 RESEARCH ON BILINGUALISM
L'University Laval
P.O. Box 2447
Quebec, Canada

INTERNATIONAL READING
 ASSOCIATION
800 Barksdale Road
Newark, DE 19711

JAPAN INFORMATION SERVICE
280 Park Ave.
New York, NY 10017
Contact: Consulate General of
 Japan

JAPANESE AMERICAN CURRICULUM
  PROJECT, INC. (Title VII)
414 East Third Ave.
P.O. Box 367
San Mateo, CA 94401
(415) 343-9408

THE LEARNING TREE
9998 Ferguson Road
Dallas, TX 75228

LIBRARIES UNLIMITED
Box 263
Littleton, CO 80120

LIBRARY OF CONGRESS
1st & Independence Ave., SE
Washington, DC 20540
(202) 287-5000

MAGEN DAVID YESHIVA (Hebrew)
50 Ave. "P"
Brooklyn, NY 11204
(212) 236-5905
Contact: Bonnie Hendel

MICHIGAN ETHNIC HERITAGE
  STUDIES CENTER
Wayne State University
197 Manoogian Hall
Detroit, MI 48202

MIDWEST OFFICE FOR MATERIALS
  DEVELOPMENT (Vietnamese)
805 West Pennsylvania Ave.,
  3rd Floor
University of Illinois
Urbana, IL 61801
(217) 333-2615

MOUNTAIN VIEW-LOS ALTOS
  UNIFIED HIGH SCHOOL DISTRICT
  (Title VII, Ilokano)
1299 Bryant St.
Mountain View, CA 94040
(415) 967-5543
Contact: Robert McLennan

MULTICULTURAL RESOURCES
Box 2945
Stanford, CA 94305

NATIONAL ASSESSMENT AND
  DISSEMINATION CENTER (TITLE
  VII)
385 High Street
Fall River, MA 02720

NATIONAL ASSESSMENT OF
  EDUCATION PROGRESS
Education Commission of the
  States
1860 Lincoln St., Suite 700
Denver, CO 80295

NATIONAL ASSOCIATION FOR
  BILINGUAL EDUCATION (NABE)
IU-13 BESL Center
100 Franklin St.
New Holland, PA 17557
(717) 354-7737
Contact: Ramon L. Santiago

NATIONAL ASSOCIATION FOR EQUAL
  OPPORTUNITY IN HIGHER
  EDUCATION
2001 S St., NW
Washington, DC 20009
(202) 232-8500

NATIONAL ASSOCIATION OF
 INTERDISCIPLINARY ETHNIC
 STUDIES
101 Main Hall
University of Wisconsin-La
 Crosse
La Crosse, WI 54601

NATIONAL ASSOCIATION OF
 MEXICAN AMERICAN EDUCATORS
2717 Winthrop Ave.
Arcadia, CA 91006
(213) 245-1000

THE NATIONAL CENTER FOR
 RESEARCH IN VOCATIONAL
 EDUCATION
The Ohio State University
1960 Kenny Road
Columbus, OH 43210

NATIONAL CENTER FOR URBAN
 ETHNIC AFFAIRS
1521 16th Street, NW
Washington, DC

NATIONAL CLEARINGHOUSE FOR
 BILINGUAL EDUCATION
1500 Wilson Boulevard, Suite
 802
Rosslyn, VA 22209
(703) 522-0710 or Hot Line
 (800) 336-4560

NATIONAL CONFERENCE OF
 CHRISTIANS AND JEWS
43 W. 57th Street
New York, NY

NATIONAL COUNCIL FOR
 ACCREDITATION OF TEACHER
 CERTIFICATION
1750 Pennylvania Ave., NW,
 Suite 411
Washington, DC 20006

NATIONAL COUNCIL OF TEACHERS
 OF ENGLISH
1111 Kenyon Road
Urbana, IL 61801

NATIONAL EDUCATION ASSOCIATION
1201 16th Street, NW
Washington, DC 20036
(202) 833-4000

NATIONAL EDUCATION LAB
 PUBLICATIONS
813 Airport Blvd.
Austin, TX 78708

THE NATIONAL FOUNDATION FOR
 THE IMPROVEMENT OF EDUCATION
1156 15th Street, NW, Suite
 918
Washington, DC 20005

NATIONAL INDIAN EDUCATION
 ASSOCIATION
3036 University Ave., SE
Minneapolis, MN 55414

NATIONAL INDOCHINESE
 CLEARINGHOUSE AND TECHNICAL
 ASSISTANCE CENTER (NIC/TAC)
Center for Applied Linguistics
1611 North Kent St.
Arlington, VA 22209
(703) 528-4312 or Hot Line
 (800) 336-3040
Contact: Allene G. Grognet

NATIONAL INSTITUTE OF
 EDUCATION
U. S. Department of HEW
Washington, DC 20208

THE NATIONAL HUMANITIES
 FACULTY
1266 Main Street
Concord, MA 01742

NATIONAL ORGANIZATION OF WOMEN
 (NOW)
425 13th St.
Washington, DC
(202) 347-2279

NATIONAL SUPPORT SYSTEMS
 PROJECT
253 Burton Hall
University of Minnesota
Minneapolis, MN 55455
(612) 373-4854
Contact: Maynard C. Reynolds

NATIONAL TASK FORCE ON
 DESEGREGATION STRATEGIES
Education Commission of the
 States
1860 Lincoln St., Suite 300
Denver, CO 80295
(303) 861-4917
Contact: Ben Williams,
 Director

NATIONAL TITLE VII
 DISSEMINATION AND ASSESSMENT
 CENTER
California State University,
 Los Angeles
5151 State University Dr.
Los Angeles, CA 90032

NATIVE AMERICAN MATERIALS
 DEVELOPMENT CENTER (Title
 VII)
407 Rio Grande Boulevard, NW
Albuquerque, NM 87104
(505) 242-5222
Contact: Gloria Emerson,
 Director

NEW ENGLAND
 MULTILINGUAL-MULTICULTURAL
 TEACHING RESOURCE CENTER,
 (Title VII)
Bilingual Program
86 Fourth St.
Povidence, RI 02906
(401) 272-4900, exts. 293, 297

OFFICE FOR ADVANCEMENT OF
 PUBLIC NEGRO COLLEGES
National Association of State
 Universities & Land-Grant
 Colleges
805 Peachtree St., NE
Atlanta, GA 30308
(404) 874-8073

OFFICE OF COPYRIGHT
Copyright Office
Library of Congress
Washington, DC 20559
(703) 557-8700

ONTARIO INSTITUTE FOR STUDIES
 IN EDUCATION
252 Bloor Street West
Toronto, Ontario M5S 1V6

ORGANIZATION OF AMERICAN
 STATES
General Secretariat
17th St., NW, at Constitution
 Ave.
Washington, DC 20006
(202) 789-3000

PACIFIC ASIAN LANGUAGE
 MATERIALS DEVELOPMENT CENTER
 (Title VII)
Portues 713B
2424 Maile Way
Honolulu, HI 96734

PEER (PROJECT ON EQUAL
 EDUCATION RIGHTS)
NOW Legal Defense & Education
 Fund
1029 Vermont Ave., NW, Suite
 800
Washington, DC 20005
(202) 332-7337
Contact: Holly Knox

PINELLAS COUNTY SCHOOLS (Title
 VII)
Curriculum and Instruction
 Center
205 4th St., SW
Largo, FL 33540
(813) 585-9951
Contact: Maria Sanchez

PRAEGER SPECIAL STUDIES
383 Madison Ave.
New York, NY 10017

PROJECT BEST
Bilingual Education Applied
 Research Unit
Hunter College
560 Lexington Ave.
New York, NY 10022
Contact: Marietta Saravia
 Shore, Coordinator

R & E RESEARCH ASSOCIATES,
 INC.
936 Industrial Ave.
Palo Alto, CA 94303

RESOURCE CENTER FOR ITALIAN
 (Title VII)
Public School #97
Ave. "S" & Stillwell Ave.
Brooklyn, NY 11223
(212) 372-7393
Contact: Mrs. Paul Alleva

RESOURCE CENTER FOR RUSSIAN
 (Title VII)
Public School #225
1075 Oceanview Ave.
Brooklyn, NY 11235
(212) 743-9793 or 266-1733
Contact: Emil Bednar or Gina
 Sullivan

RESOURCE AND REFERRAL SERVICE
 (Part of the Research &
 Development Exchange,
 National Institute of
 Education)
The Ohio State University
1960 Kenny Road
Columbus, OH 43210
(614) 486-3655
Contact: John C. Peterson

ROMANIAN LIBRARY
200 East 38th St.
New York, NY 10016
Contact: Ion Monafu,
 Executive Secretary

THE SCHOMBURG CENTER FOR
 RESEARCH IN BLACK CULTURE
103 West 135th St.
New York, NY 10030
(212) 862-4000
Contact: Otillia Pearson

SOCIAL SCIENCE EDUCATION
 CONSORTIUM
855 Broadway
Boulder, CO 80203

SOUTH SHORE HIGH SCHOOL (Title
 VII, Russian)
Bilingual Education
6565 Flatlands Ave.
Brooklyn, NY 11236
(212) 531-4454
Contact: Anna Elman

SOUTHERN REGIONAL EDUCATION
  BOARD
130 Sixth Street, NW
Atlanta, GA 30313

SPEECH COMMUNICATION
  ASSOCIATION
5205 Leesburg Pike, Suite 1000
Falls Church, VA 22041
(703) 879-1888

SPRINT
Women's Equity Action League
Educational & Legal Defense
  Fund
805 Fifteenth St., NW, Suite
  822
Washington, DC 20005
(202) 638-1961
Contact: Margaret Beck-Rex

STUDENT NATIONAL EDUCATION
  ASSOCIATION
1201 16th St., NW
Washington, DC 20036
(202) 833-5525

SUPPLIERS OF SPANISH-LANGUAGE
  MATERIALS
American Library Association
Adults Services
Division Subcommittee on
  Spanish Materials
50 East Huron St.
Chicago, Il 60611

TEACHERS OF ENGLISH TO
  SPEAKERS OF OTHER LANGUAGES
  (T.E.S.O.L.)
455 Nevils Building
Georgetown University
Washington, DC 20057

TELECOMMUNICATIONS CONSUMER
  COALITION
105 Madison Ave., Suite 921
New York, NY 10016
(212) 683-5656
Contact: Ralph M. Jennings,
  Executive Director

TITLE VII ASSESSMENT AND
  DISSEMINATION CENTER
  (Includes Pacific Area
  Languages)
California State University -
  Los Angeles
5151 State University Drive
Los Angeles, CA 90032
(213) 224-3676
Contact: Charles Leyba

TITLE VII ESEA BILINGUAL
  PROJECT
Seattle Public Schools
520 Ravenna Boulevard, NE
Seattle, WA 98115
Contact: Janet Lu, Project
  Director

TONATIUH INTERNATIONAL
2150 Shattuck Avenue
Berkeley, CA 94704

TULARE COUNTY DEPARTMENT OF
  EDUCATION (Title VII)
Education Building, County
  Civic Center
Visalia, CA 98277
(209) 733-6681 or 733-6606
Contact: Robert Aguilar

THE UNITED NATIONS ASSOCIATION
  OF THE USA
345 East 46th St.
New York, NY 10017
(212) 697-3232

THE UNITED NATIONS
Information Office, DC 1930
New York, NY 10017
(212) 754-1234

U. S. GOVERNMENT PRINTING
 OFFICE
710 North Capitol, NW
Washington, DC 20402
(202) 783-3238

U. S. OFFICE OF EDUCATION
Equal Education Opportunity
 Programs
Bureau of Elementary and
 Secondary Education
400 Maryland Ave., SW, Room
 2001
Washington, DC 20202
(202) 245-8484

U. S. BUREAU OF INDIAN
 AFFAIRS
U.S. Department of the
 Interior
1951 Constitution Ave., NW, Rm
 3510
Washington, DC 20245
(202) 343-2123

U. S. DIVISION OF JOB
 PLACEMENT
Bureau of Indian Affairs,
 U.S. Department of the
 Interior
1951 Constitution Ave., NW,
 Rm. 4555
Washington, DC 20245
(202) 343-7408

U. S. OFFICE OF BILINGUAL
 EDUCATION
Division of Program
 Development
U.S. Office of Education
Reporters Building, Rm. 421
300 7th St., SW
Washington, DC 20202
(202) 447-9227

U. S. OFFICE OF INDIAN
 EDUCATION
U.S. Office of Education
400 Maryland Ave., SW,
 Rm. 2161
Washington, DC 20202
(202) 245-7525

U. S. OFFICE OF EDUCATION,
 RESEARCH AND DEMONSTRATION
 DIVISION
Bureau of Occupational & Adult
 Education
GSA Regional Office Building
 3, Room 5042
7th & D Sts., SW
Washington, DC 20202
(202) 245-9634

U. S. DIVISION OF
 INTERNATIONAL EDUCATION
U.S. Office of Education
GSA Regional Office Building
 3, Room 3919
7th & D Sts., SW
Washington, DC 20202
(202) 245-2293

U. S. READING ACADEMIES
 PROGRAM RIGHT TO READ
U.S. Office of Education
400 Maryland Ave., SW, Room
 1154
Donohoe Building
Washington, DC 20202
(202) 245-8213

U. S. TEACHER CENTERS PROGRAM
U.S. Office of Education
400 Maryland Ave.
Washington, DC 20202
(202) 653-5843

U. S. WOMEN'S EQUITY PROGRAM
U.S. Office of Education
400 Maryland Ave., SW, Room 3121
Washington, DC 20202
(202) 245-2181

UNIVERSITY OF HAWAII (Title VII, Korean)
Department of ESL
1890 East West Road
Honolulu, HI 96822
(808) 948-8814
Contact: Donald M. Topping, Director

URBAN COLLEGE AND UNIVERSITY NETWORK
One Dupont Circle, Suite 700
Washington, DC 20036
(202) 293-7070
Contact: Kurt B. Smith, Network Coodinator

VOICES FROM THE EARTH
Yonahwaylut
c/o Akwesasne Notes
Mohawk Nation
Rooseveltown, NY 13683
(518) 483-2540
Contact: Mike Myers

WOMEN'S ACTION ALLIANCE
370 Lexington Ave.
New York, NY 10017
(212) 685-0800

WEECN (WOMEN'S EDUCATIONAL EQUITY COMMUNICATIONS NETWORK)
Far West Laboratory for Educational Research & Development
1855 Folsom St.
San Francisco, CA 94103
(415) 565-3000

WOMEN'S EQUITY ACTION LEAGUE EDUCATIONAL AND LEGAL DEFENSE FUND (WEAL FUND)
National Press Building
Washington, DC 20045
(202) 638-4560

WORLD BANK PUBLICATIONS
1818 H St., NW
Washington, DC 20433
(202) 477-1234

YUBA CITY UNIFIED SCHOOL DISTRICT (Title VII, Punjabi)
Bilingual Program
243 Colusa Ave.
Yuba City, CA 95991
(916) 674-0751
Contact: Paul McIntire

AUTHOR INDEX

Name	Page
Abbey, Karin	7
Acosta, Oscar Zeta	57
Ahlum, Carol	61
Alcala, Consuelo	49
Allen, Judy	69
Almance, Sofia	72
Almeida, Raymond A.	51
American Assembly	15
American College Testing Program (ACT)	43
American Council on Education	43
American Institutes for Research	43
Anderson, Grace M.	76
Anderson, Theodore	14
Angelou, Maya	57
Anti-Defamation League of B'nai B'rith	14
Aoki, Ted	14
Arciniega, Tomas A.	14
Arnow, Beth	15
Asia Society	15
Asian American Bilingual Education Center	61
Austin, Nancy	31
Bagley, Christopher	15
Baker, Gwendolyn C.	15, 20
Baker, William P.	76
Bales, Carol Ann	51
Banks, James A.	15, 16, 95
Banks, Henry A.	62
Baptiste, H. Prentice, Jr.	16, 61
Baptiste, Mira L.	16, 61
Barnhardt, Ray	16
Baroni, Geno	17, 37
Barrett, Leonard E.	51
Barrio, Raymond	57
Bass, Kathy	10
Beckoff, Samuel	60
Beckum, Leonard D.	62
Benitez, Mario A.	3
Berbrich, Joan D.	53
Berry, Mary F.	17
Beuf, Ann H.	17
Black Studies Program	62
Blaze, Wayne	3
Blourock, Barbara	30
Blumenberg, Eleanor	98
Boberg, Alice	65
Bogle, Donald	51
Bowman, James	30
Boyer, James B.	17
Boyer, Joe L.	17
Boyer, Mildred	14
Boykin, William C.	77
Brandhorst, Ted	12
Brazziel, William F.	17
Britton, Gwyneth	43
Brooks, Dennis	76
Brown, Gaile	23
Brownson, Charles B.	38
Buckalwe, L. W.	51
Buergenthal, Thomas	18
Bullock, Charles S. III	96
Burry, James	44
Butler, Katie B.	62
Buu, Tri	63
California State Department of Education	4
Calvin, Richmond	4
Canadian Ministry of Education	63
Cardenas, Jose A.	4
Carkhuff, Robert R.	63
Carnegie Council on Policy Studies in Education	18
Carter, Clifford	98
Casso, Henry J.	18
Castaneda, Alfredo	18
Casteel, J. Doyle	63
Chaffee, Fonda L.	96
Chan, Jeffery Paul	57
Chin, Frank	57
Chinweizu	51
Chisholm, Shirley	57
Chow, Stanley H. L.	62
Cobbs, Price M.	19

Coffin, Gregory C.........44
Cohen, David...............4
Colangelo, Nicholas.......19
Cole, Ann.................63
Cole, Katherine...........38
Commission for
  Racial Equality.........19
Community Relations
  Commission..............19
Cooper, Clare M...........53
Cordasco, Francesco.......52
Cortes, Carlos E......20, 64,
                      96, 98
Cotera, Martha P.......5, 35
Council on Interracial
  Books for Children......44
Coursen, David............99
Coye, Molly Joel..........52
Cross, Dolores E..........20
Cross, William E., Jr.....76
Cullinan, Bernice E.......20
Daniel, Jack L............20
Daniel, Philip T. K.......44
Daniels, Deborah K........21
Darnell, Frank............21
Davidson, R. Theodore.....21
Dawson, Martha E..........21
Dequera, Alida............54
Diop, Cheikh Anna.........52
Dissemination and Assess-
  ment Center for
  Bilingual Education......5
Donant, Franklyn D........68
Downs, Ray F..............52
Duran, Daniel Flores.......5
Dustin, Dick..............19
Earhart, Connie...........64
Ehrlich, Rosalie..........32
EPIE Institute.............6
Elazar, Daniel............21
Erdoes, Ricard E..........52
ERIC/CRESS.................6
Eterovich, Adam S..........6
Evans, G. Edward...........7
Ferguson, Henry...........64
Fersh, Seymour............64
Fischel, Andrew...........31
Foxley, Cecelia H.........19
Fralley, Jacqueline.......61
Franco, John M............64
Frazier, Nancy............32

Friedman, Murray..........21
Froschl, Merle.............7
Fuchigami, Robert Y.......38
Gage, Alfred..............64
Gallagher, Buell G........44
Galli, Marcia J...........54
Gappa, Judith M...........22
Gay, Geneva...............95
Gentry, Harold W..........96
Giese, James...............7
Giles, Raymond H..........22
Gold, Milton J............22
Golden, Edna T............65
Gollnick, Donna M..........4,
            16, 26, 39, 65, 76
Gonzales, Joe R............7
Gordon, Fannetta N........63
Gorena, Minerva...........65
Grabowski, John J.........65
Grant, Carl...........22, 23
Grant, Gloria.............66
Green, Gerson.............17
Griffin, Leslie J.........68
Gumina, Deanna Paoli......53
Gunther, Lenworth.........53
Haas, Carolyn.............63
Hagel, Phyllis.............7
Hall, Gene E..............23
Hall, Mary................91
Hall, Morrill M...........96
Hall, Ron.................77
Hallman, Clemens L........63
Halperin, Michael.........23
Hansen-Krening, Nancy.....66
Harley, Elsie F...........44
Harley, Sharon............24
Haro, Carlos Manuel.......24
Hart, Elinor...............8
Hartley, Mary ELizabeth...24
Haskins, James............53
Hausman, Gerald...........57
Hawaii Bilingual/Bicultural
  Education Project.......66
Hawaii State Instruc-
  tional Services.........45
Healey, Sally A...........53
Hecht, Marie B............53
Heisley, Michael...........7
Heller, Elizabeth.........63
Hernandez, Elida..........66
Higgs, David..............76

Hill, Barbara T..........66
Hilliard, Asa G..........45
Hinds, Charles F.........39
Hodges, Norman E. W......54
Holt International
  Children's Service.....67
Hoopes, David S...22, 24, 25
Hord, Shirley............23
Howard, Suzanne......67, 77
Hsu, Kai-yu..............58
Hunter, Kathleen A.......15
Husen, Torsten...........98
Hunter, William A....25, 77
Illinois Office of
  Education..............67
Inada, Lawson Fusao......57
Inglehart, Babette F......8
Israel, William I........25
Jackson, Curtis E........54
James, Richard L.........18
Japanese American
  Citizens League........67
Jaramillo, Mari-Luci.....25
Jefferson, Margo.........68
Jensen, Henry C..........76
Johnson, Sylvia T........46
Johnson, Willis L........39
Jones, Reginald L........25
Katz, Jane B.............58
Kennicott, Patrick C......8
King, Edith W..........8, 25
Klassen, Frank H.........26
Kohls, Robert L..........26
Kotler, Greta.............8
Kovac, Roberta...........68
Krathwohl, David.........94
Kuncaitis, Violetta.......8
Kuvlesky, William P......77
Lambers, Gail............36
Lamy, Steven L...........68
Lawson, John D...........68
Leavitt, Howard B........26
Ledee, Marcos............54
Levinsohn, Florence H....26
Levy, Jack.............8, 65
Leyba, Charles F........8, 9
Lincoln, Eugene A........78
Lippitt, Gordon L........22
Liu, Wu-Chi..............58
Livingston, Jon..........52
Lo, Irving Yucheng.......58
Locks, Nancy A...........46
Logan, Louisette.........63
Longstreet, Wilma S......27
Lopez, Ronald W..........27
Lumpkin, Margaret........43
Lynch, Robert............68
MacCracken, Mary.........58
Macias, Reynoldo Flores..27
Madrid-Barela, Arturo....27
Mallea, John R............9
Mangione, Anthony R.......8
Mankato Minority Group
  Studies Center..........9
des Marais, Philip.......93
Mathieson, Moria B........9
Matthews, Martha.........69
May, William H...........30
McCormack, Wayne.........27
McCune, Shirley..........69
McCunn, Ruthanne Lum.....54
McNamara, Donna B........69
McNeill, Earldene....11, 69
Miaso, Jozef.............54
Michael, John A..........40
Michigan Ethnic Heritage
  Studies Center.........69
Midura, Edmund M.........27
Midwest Center for
  Equal Educational
  Opportunity.............9
Ministry of Education,
  Canada.................10
Miron, Murray............30
Mitchell, Gertrude.......96
Mohr, Paul...............28
Momaday, N. Scott........70
Montalvo, David..........54
Moore, Robert B..........70
Morris, Lee..............28
Murakishi, Linda J.......15
Murphy, Sharon...........55
Murray, John.............28
Muse, Ivan D.............29
National Advisory Council
  on Black Higher Educa-
  tion & Black Colleges
  & Universities......46, 78
National Advisory Council
  on Women's Educational
  Programs...............29

National Alliance of
  Businessmen...............39
National Assessment of
  Educational Progress.....46
National Audiovisual
  Center, National Ar-
  chives & Records.........10
National Conference of
  Christians & Jews........29
National Council for
  Accreditation of
  Teacher Education........47
National Dissemination
  and Assessment Center
  for Bilingual Education..58
National Education
  Association..............47
National Indian Education
  Association..............70
National Indochinese
  Clearinghouse............71
National Institute of
  Education....29, 30, 40, 78
Nero, John....................3
Newton, James E.............47
Nicholas, A. X..............59
Nichols, Margaret......5, 10
Noar, Gertrude..............47
Nyhan, Patricia.............51
Office of the
  Federal Register.........40
Oliver, Thomas..............67
O'Neill, Peggy..............10
Orlich, Donald C............90
Orlich, Patricia Rend.....90
Orozco, Cecillo.............48
Osayande, Kobla, I. M.....65
Osgood, Charles E..........30
Otero, George G......71, 72
Pantoja, Antonia............30
Park, Jeanne S..............71
Pasternak, Michael G......71
Payne, Charles..............98
Pederson, Paul B............24
Peterson, Reece L...........10
Phelps, Stanlee.............31
Phi Delta Kappa.............48
Pifer, Alan.................31
Platt, Kin..................59
Pletcher, Barbara A........46
Plotch, Walter..............34

Plotz, Helen................59
Pierce, Richard.............63
Pottker, Janice.............31
Pratte, Richard.............31
President's Commision on
  Foreign Language and
  International Studies.....
                      31, 32
Project PAIUTE.............72
Pulles, Patrice.............10
Purushothaman, M............11
Pusch, Margaret D...........32
Rasmussen, Karen.............4
Reed, Dennis.................7
Renwick, George W...........24
Reynolds, Dorothy...........46
Rhodes, Bessie M. L........44
Rivlin, Harry N.............22
Rizzo, Diane................49
Roach, Hildred..............55
Robbins, Webster............18
Robinson, William H........59
Rodrigues, Raymond J.......99
Rosen, Kenneth..............59
Rosenfelt, Deborah
  Silverton................11
Sadker, David...............48
Sadker, Myra..........32, 48
Safferston, Mark J.........69
St. John, Nancy H...........99
Salas, Isabel...............15
Salazar, Theresa............11
Samora, Julian..............72
Sandstrom, Eleanor....33, 54
Santos-Rivera, Iris........49
Sather, Greg................28
Scherer, Joseph J..........69
Schlitt, Ann M..............15
Schmidt, Velma E......11, 69
Schull, Susan...............28
Schulman, Jay...............32
Schwarz-Bart, Andre........60
Schweitzer, Frederick M...56
Schwier, Richard............68
Seitz, Victoria.............32
Servin, Manuel P...........56
Shatter, Aubrey.............32
Shea, Edward C...............9
Shoemaker, Francis.........33
Shuman, Pamela..............23
Simon, Patricia Vandel....72

Simonson, Michael R.	32
Singh, Karamjit	76
Skinner, Elliot P.	68
Slawshk, Dorothy A.	12
Smiley-Marquez, Carolyn	11
Smith, Gary R.	72
Smith, Mona	68
Social Science Education Consortium	48
Sotomayor, Frank	33, 78
Spache, George D.	12
Spencer, Maria	72
Sprung, Barbara	73
Standing Bear, Luther	56
Standley, Nancy V.	79
Stein, Elaine	68
Stepp, Emma Gonzalez	35
Sterling, Dorothy	56
Stewart, Edward C.	33
Stiles, Lindley J.	20
Student National Education Association	73
Sutman, Francis X.	33
Taylor, Alvin Leon	62, 73
Terborg-Penn, Rosalyn	24
Thompson, Thomas	34
Tiedt, Pamela L.	73
Tiedt, Iris M.	73
Tittle, Carol Kehr	49
Tolzmann, Don Heinrich	12
Tomasi, S. M.	37
Torney, Judith	18
Torrance, E. Paul	34
Torres, George A.	12
Trueblood, Felicity M.	63
Tumin, Melvin M.	34
Turner, William H.	40
U.S. Commission on Civil Rights	34, 35, 41
U.S. Congress	41
Universal Esperanto Association	35
University Center for International Studies	12
Uribe, Oscar J., Jr.	62
Urzua, Roberto	35
Valencia, Atilano A.	36
Valverde, Leonard A.	74
Ventura, Paul	25
Villarreal, Lupita	3
Von Euler, Mary	36
Wagen, Robert	74
Washburn, David E.	41
Washington, William D.	60
Weibust, Patricia	74
Weinberg, Meyer	36
Weinberger, Betty	63
Weitzman, Lenore J.	49
Wenk, Michael	37
Williams, Byron	49
Williamson, Jane	7
Winokur, Diane K.	19
Westoff, Leslie Aldridge	37
Wise, James H.	37
Women on Words and Images	49
Women's Studies Program	74
Wong, Shawn Hsu	57
Wood, Dean D.	75
Wright, Benjamin D.	26
Wroblewski, Ralph	65
Wynar, Anna T.	14, 41
Wynar, Lubomyer	14, 41
Wynn, Cordell	51
Zak, Judith Zielinski	65
Zurawski, Joseph W.	13